TALES FROM UNDER THE RIM

THE MARKETING OF TIM HORTONS

TALES FROM UNDER THE RIM

THE MARKETING OF TIM HORTONS

RON BUIST

Edited by Susan Renouf and Laurel Boone.
Cover image by Peter Tym.
Author photo by Ted Brellisford / Courtsey of *The Hamilton Spectator*.
Cover design by Kevin Buist and Paul Vienneau.
Book design by Paul Vienneau.
Photographs appearing on pages 28, 38, 42, 68, 72, 184, 186, 188, 190, and 194 have been reproduced with the permission of the TDL Group Corp. / Tim Hortons (TDL). Photographs on pages 36, 50, 78, 86, 92, 130, 142, 148, 158, 164, 172, 176, 178, and 204 are by Ron Buist (RB).

Printed in Canada by Friesens.
10 9 8 7 6 5 4 3 2 1

NATIONAL LIBRARY OF CANADA CATALOGUING IN PUBLICATION

Buist, Ron
Tales from under the rim: the marketing of Tim Hortons / Ron Buist.

Includes index.
ISBN 0-86492-365-1

1. Tim Hortons Ltd. — History. 2. Buist, Ron I. Title.

TX945.5.T54B84 2003 338.7'61647957 C2003-903894-7

Published with the financial support of the Canada Council for the Arts, the Government of Canada through the Book Publishing Industry Development Program, and the New Brunswick Culture and Sports Secretariat.

Contents and opinions in this book are those of the author, and not those of the TDL Group Corp. / Tim Hortons.

For speaking engagements, contact the National Speakers Bureau at 800-661-4110 or speakers@nsb.com.

GOOSE LANE EDITIONS
469 King Street
Fredericton, New Brunswick
CANADA E3B 1E5
www.gooselane.com

This book is dedicated to Tim Hortons customers,
who made Tim Hortons their own.

Table of Contents

Acknowledgements

WRITING A BOOK OF THIS NATURE involves a lot of help from so many. In over two years of putting this book together, all of the following people became part of my story. Through recollections, phone conversations, and personal interviews, they all have helped to make this book a reality, thereby helping me preserve one of Canada's greatest business success stories. Most of these people are mentioned in the following chapters, with their proper titles and experiences. All are important, and if any are not mentioned directly, it's because they supplied some of the background material and gave personal assistance.

With the exception of Ron Joyce, I have listed everyone alphabetically. Without Ron, there would be no Tim Hortons story.

The following members of the Tim Hortons executive gave of their time, their thoughts, or, through my recollections, their strong desire to make Tim Hortons such a success: Paul House, Patti Jameson, Alf Lane, Bill Moir, Don Schroeder, and Henry Svazas.

Store owners, past and present TDL staff, family members of the company — they are all to be thanked for their help or through their remembered contributions over the years: Michele Allison, Sharon Cook, Eldon Fawcett, Fred Falconer, Ron Fitchett, Jim Flemming, Len Graham, Linda Grieve, Stan Hare, John Hoey, Art and Joan Jenkins, Grace Joyce, Jeri-Lynn Horton Joyce, Bud Kennish, Bruce Leckie, John Lynn, the Mattatalls — Ed, Florence, Miles, Chris and Ryan; Peter Moffat, D'Arcy and Barbara Murphy, Gary and Mary O'Neill, Graham Oliver, Kerri Lynn McArthur, Kathie McPhee, George McGlinchey, Paul Preuss, Wesley Rafuse, Sandy and Bev Shearer, Alec and Wilma Strom, and Gary and Karen Wilson.

And in memory of Tim and Lori Horton and Willard (Bill) Joyce.

It takes more than those employed directly with the company to make it work. I want to thank the following people, whose specific contributions, both big and small, either to my personal career or directly to Hortons, are part of this book: the Blacks — Eddie, Bill, Bob, Barry, and Bruce; Terri Black, Spencer Brown, Michael Cerny, Bill Cluff, Jim Charade, Trevor Collier, Dennis Griggs, Jeannine Hillier, Bill Huntley, Barry (B.J.) Jones, Jack Kuper, Donna Lloyd, Natalie MacMaster, Darcy Maloney, Angelo Mosca, Don MacKay, Donna McPhail, Barry McSween, Joanne Stewart, Pat Quinn, David Wallen, Casey Weilhower, and Roger Wilson. I am especially grateful to Barry Van Horn, who always emphasized staying focused on the desired result. "Just write the book, Ron, write the damn book," he would say, and I did. Thanks, Barry.

Two companies deserve special mention for their "behind the scenes" support. An article in *Marketing Magazine* first got me interested in Hortons, and when this book was going together, Jim McElguinn, formerly with *Marketing Magazine*, responded again and again to my phone calls for historical clarification; as well, *Marketing Magazine* reported on my book venture. When I needed help with a specially designed hot drink cup to promote this book, Mary Legge, Jason Monck, and Don Bell of Conference Cup came through, as they always do with Hortons cups, on time and magnificently.

I am most grateful to my publisher, Susanne Alexander, of Goose Lane Editions, for believing in my book and giving me the opportunity to share my memories. I owe special thanks to Susan Renouf, my initial editor, who performed literary surgery on my manuscript and added her advice and suggestions while exercising a heavy-duty blue pencil. Laurel Boone, Editorial Director of Goose Lane Editions, used her expertise to make my manuscript into a book, and Paul Vienneau worked diligently on the interior and exterior design of the book.

Above all, I offer my heartfelt thanks to my wife, Mary Ann, Kevin, our son, who did the initial design for the book cover and promotional cup, and Suzanne, our daughter. They lived these times just as much as I did, and they supported my crazy ideas and my ups and downs over all the years.

And special thanks to my friend, John Green, for always being there.

"The kind of business to get into is selling
a consumable product that everybody wants."
— William J. (Bill) Huntley, Vice President Finance,
Black Photo Limited (retired)

This cartoon was first published in *The Montreal Monitor*. © STAN ROACH

PROLOGUE

Walking Miss Lillian to the Top of the Hill

PLAY A WORD GAME WITH ME.

If I say "service station," what comes to mind? Probably "a place to buy gas." The phrase "service station" doesn't say anything about gas, but after years of hearing it, we just recognize that a service station is a business that sells gas.

Try this one: "air conditioning" — "cool air," right? Somebody, somewhere, at some time thought the phrase "air conditioning" would be an appealing way to say "cool air," and now that's our automatic understanding of the term.

Here's another: "Tim Hortons." Yes, the instant association is "coffee," and has been for many years. In 1996, though, after I had been working in the Tim Hortons marketing department for over thirteen years, I wondered, why was Tim Hortons so closely associated with coffee? Although sales of our coffee exceeded the coffee sales of all our competitors, we also sold uniquely fresh and tasty donuts. Our Timbits had become so popular that "Timbit" had almost become a generic term. Our soups, sandwiches, cakes, and pies had become national favourites. Yet our coffee remained our number-one attraction. How could we best define this success in advertising that would encapsulate the excellence of our products and our stores?

To help develop a picture of our success, my colleague Bill Moir, Executive Vice President of Marketing, introduced me to Trevor Collier Research, a professional market research company. We wanted to know, not just what our own customers liked and disliked, but also what the customers of our competitors had to say about us. Trevor Collier took us across Canada, conducting focus groups everywhere we went. The groups consisted of people who bought "a cup of coffee from a coffee shop every day, once a week, or once a month." These men and women sat with a moderator around a table in a room with a panel of one-way glass. Seated behind this glass, we could watch them and listened to their comments without disturbing their concentration. Each group discussed both Tim Hortons and our competitors. At the end of the evening, we asked the members to tell us how they would define Tim Hortons in general and, more specifically, Tim Hortons coffee.

What a surprise these generous people gave us. They liked the coffee's flavour, they liked its freshness, they liked the consistency of our service. But they didn't relate only to flavour, freshness, and service. Tim Hortons coffee, they told us, was actually a part of their lives. Going to one of our stores for a coffee break was part of their daily ritual. We heard about a woman in labour who insisted that her husband take her through the drive-through to get a Tim Hortons coffee en route to the hospital. We heard from expectant fathers who needed their Tim Hortons coffee before heading for the delivery room. We found some stories hard to accept, but one of the strangest proved to be true: a man wrote in his will that his funeral cortège was to go through the Tim Hortons drive-through, and all members of the funeral party were to have a cup of coffee, on him. One member of the Halifax focus group explained in careful detail about an elderly lady who, each day, would walk with her cane up the hill from her house to Tim Hortons for her morning coffee. It was part of her daily ritual, part of her life, our informant said. She always had time for Tim Hortons.

Our focus group sessions produced two dramatic changes for Tim Hortons. First, "You've always got time for Tim Hortons" became our advertising slogan. Second, Lillian, the elderly lady who walked up the hill to Tim's, became the star of the first of our "True Stories" television advertising campaigns. The commercial featured Lillian herself and a Tim Hortons store outside Lunenburg, Nova Scotia; her own Lunenburg store was just too small for all the production gear and crew. This commercial embodied the warmth and friendliness people described to us in their stories about Tim Hortons. Between 1996 and 2001, nine True Stories were filmed, and they are still being produced from stories submitted by our customers and store owners. The combination of excellent products and neighbourly stores so treasured by the participants in our focus groups became the heart of the Tim Hortons marketing program.

A cartoon from *The Halifax Chronicle-Herald*. BRUCE MacKINNON / ARTIZANS.COM

CHAPTER ONE

Grabbing the Tail of a Comet

NOVEMBER 13, 1977.
9:00 a.m.

I have been in my new office at Tim Hortons for half an hour. It's my first day on the job. The phone rings — my first phone call.

"Are you the advertising manager?"

"That's right."

"Where is it?"

"Where is what, sir?"

"The advertising."

I remember that first call as if it happened yesterday. My caller was Gary O'Neill, the largest single franchisee in Eastern Canada, who had several stores in Moncton, New Brunswick. He had not received any advertising from head office for several months. He had been paying into the store owners' national advertising fund, and he expected to see some results. Made sense to me. When I investigated the situation, I found out that, since no one had been running the marketing department, the money had not been going anywhere. The advertising fund contributions had accumulated in the bank, while six months' worth of unpaid bills for the seventy-nine-store chain had accumulated in the "in" basket that now belonged to me.

My office consisted of solid brick walls on my left and behind me, a floor-to-ceiling glass wall on my right, and a glass wall in front of me punctuated by a glass door. The whole enclosure, no more than a hundred square feet in area, held one filing cabinet, three chairs (one of which I occupied), and my desk. It was nicknamed "the fish bowl."

I had been with Black's Camera Stores since 1964, when the company had fourteen stores in Ontario. Black's had started as Eddie Black's Appliances, but in 1939, Eddie Black, Sr., its founder, had an inspiration. King George VI and Queen Elizabeth visited Canada that year to drum up support for the war with Germany that seemed inevitable, and Eddie knew that the parade would go right by his store on Yonge Street in Toronto. He put a few Kodak and Bell and Howell cameras in a four-foot showcase in his store, and thus began the famous chain of camera stores.

I had worked for three years behind various Black's store counters when President Bill Black, the eldest of Eddie's four sons, asked if I would come to head office and work with Bob Black, his brother and the company's vice president. Black's had no advertising agency at that time. Bill knew that I had graduated from the Radio and TV Arts program at Ryerson Polytechnical Institute (now Ryerson University) in 1963, and that I was itching to work with their advertising program. I jumped at the chance to create and place advertising. The association was a happy one, and I stayed with Black's for thirteen years.

Black's had developed a very good photofinishing business. Their first plant was located behind one of their stores on North Yonge Street. In 1966, the plant became part of the new office building on Upjohn Road in Don Mills. In 1967, Bill Huntley, vice-president of finance, spearheaded the creation of a small pocket album in which to save the four-inch-square pictures developed from one of the popular films of the day. Both the photofinishing and the album sales were great. However, by 1972, forty per cent of all cameras sold were either Polaroids or the Kodak Instamatic type. Photofinishing lagged behind, and the machines were becoming antiquated. In those days, the average print from 35mm-film was three and a half inches wide. The rolls of paper to make these prints came in five-foot-high rolls, precut in three-and-a-half-inch strips. Bill and Bob Black, along with Bill Huntley, made a crucial and risky decision when they replaced their old machines with new ones that used four-inch-wide strips of paper. It sounds like a small change, but it had huge repercussions. All prints from Black's would now be four inches by six inches, thirty-seven per cent larger than the three-and-a-half-by-five-inch prints everyone else was producing. Black's Bigger Prints would require their own special albums; they would probably cut drastically into the five-by-seven and eight-by-ten enlargement business; and, just because they were different, they might cause a huge backlash from customers. It was a big gamble.

Black's Bigger Prints was my promotional mandate for that year. We used stock photos in our advertising pieces to omit model costs, and an outline on the new, larger print showed how much bigger it was than the old, smaller print. The consumer got more picture for the same price. Rear bus boards and newspaper and radio advertisements all over the greater Toronto area kicked off the campaign. Working with Bob Black, I learned at an early point in my career that consistency counts in advertising. The newspapers and the bus boards used the same artwork, and the advertisements were adapted into point-of-purchase advertising displayed in the stores. The visual and radio ads all broadcast the same message. We would have extended this strategy to television advertising if it had been within our budget at that time. We tied everything together, we kept the same message throughout our advertising program, and when we got it right, we restrained our urge towards creative cuteness. The strategy worked. Sales of the larger 35mm print took off, pushing the photofinishing business up forty per cent for each of the next five years. By year six, the competition finally caught up, and the four-by-six-inch print became standard.

I was not really looking for any change in my career with Black's, but one day in September, 1977, I read an article in *Marketing Magazine* that would change my life. The headline read: "Howard Resigns Horton Account." The Howard Advertising Agency had given up the advertising account of Tim Horton Donuts, of Oakville, Ontario. As I read on, I discovered that Ron Joyce, the president of Tim Donut Ltd., wanted to find someone to head up an in-house advertising department; then the company would determine what to do about advertising. I picked up the phone and called Tim Horton Donuts to see if they still had that opening for someone to "head up the advertising department."

Why? Because of my five-year-old son, Kevin. I was not pleased with the "open concept" education he was receiving in Toronto. I had grown up in Oakville. I liked the town and its amenities, and I knew the area and the school system. The idea of working in Oakville sounded good to me.

In the first week of October, I received a phone call from Linda

Grieve, Ron Joyce's secretary, asking if I could come out and meet with Mr. Joyce. We arranged a time, and I made my way to Oakville, armed with a portfolio that included audio tapes, layouts, scripts, and newspaper advertisements. I didn't realize it at the time, but the fact that I had been producing print, radio, and television advertising for Black's without the assistance of an agency proved to be very intriguing to Mr. Joyce. Black's was comparable to Tim Hortons in several ways. Both were expanding Canadian retail companies, similar in size and with similar growth patterns; Black's had grown from fourteen stores to forty-one in my time with the the company. Both were privately owned, and both produced a consumable product. Bob Black himself noted that "both Black's and Tim Hortons had the discipline to keep the stores clean, attractive and updated. Also, the staff in both systems always seemed bright and cheerful and well informed." Both companies did their advertising in-house, since neither could afford the services of an agency at that time.

That day, I met with Ron Joyce in Tim Donut Ltd.'s original office building on Sinclair Road in Oakville. It closely resembled the early Tim Horton Donut Shops: a one-storey building of dark brown brick, with a series of floor-to-ceiling gold-framed windows. The entire staff could not have been more than twenty, including the people working in the adjoining warehouse. Actually, the building was the third office for the company. The first had been in Tim Horton's home in the Don Mills area. The second was converted from a house beside store #17 on Trafalgar Road in Oakville. (This building is now a retail store under different ownership.) The location represented a compromise: Tim Horton lived in Toronto and Ron Joyce lived in Hamilton, and they split the travel distance by setting up their head office halfway between their homes. In the late 1960s, they purchased land and eventually built the offices I visited that October afternoon. This building still stands, but it is completely surrounded by the other buildings that fill the large lot the two men had bought. In addition, the company owns about two city blocks across the road. Buildings there house more office space, a store, and a 55,000-square-foot warehouse, one of six Tim Hortons now operates.

In 1977, the office building on Sinclair Road was new and designed with few private offices. One of these belonged to Ron Joyce, and that's where I first met him. I spread out the various examples of my work on his desk like a salesman spreading out his wares, looking for a sale. Ron sat behind his impressively large desk, on which sat an item that still stands out in my mind: a golden disc about the size of a quarter, mounted on an axle that allowed it to spin from front to back. On one side of the disc was a "head" and on the other a "tail." On the base, a small sign read, "Decisions, decisions." This ornament would follow him through each of his many offices as the years went on, but I never once saw him use it.

Ron was dressed in a dark blue blazer. With his no-nonsense facial expression, he carefully went over each piece I presented. I believe the fact that I did the work from creative concept to finished product myself was what intrigued him most. We discussed in particular some of the television commercials I had produced. I made these from a series of slides I had shot inside Black's stores. The slides had been reproduced on the local television station's telecine chain, a glorified movie or slide projector that could transfer the images to air or to videotape. They were accompanied by music that was in the public domain (and thus free from royalty payments), and a staff announcer did a voice-over. The particular station that aired the commercial — in this case, CHCH in Hamilton — would produce it for me as long as it ran on that station only. When the commercial was completed, I would then pack up my slides and scripts like a gypsy in the night and move on to the next station where I had purchased air time for Black's and repeat the procedure. This strategy allowed me to get Black's commercials on air without additional production cost, no small consideration for small retailers. Since the stores were concentrated at that time in a single broadcast marketing area, one advertising budget covered all twenty-four.

I particularly remember one question Ron asked me: "Do you mind flying?"

"No, I rather enjoy it."

"But do you like flying in small planes?"

"Yes, in fact some day I would like to get a pilot's license."

"That's good, because we have a small company plane for getting around." I would learn very soon just how much "getting around" there was in this job.

I had cleared the first hurdle, and so I was invited back to a meeting in the boardroom with some of the members of the executive. Unlike later Tim Hortons boardrooms, this one was in the basement. Large, paisley-patterned chesterfields that had been moved from Lori Horton's office and an oval Arborite-topped table for twelve filled what looked like an oversized living room. Questions about what I had done and why I wanted to move to Tim Hortons highlighted our conversation. I remember telling them that I was not a person who wanted to jump from job to job. Little did anyone know that, of all the men in that room that day, only one, other than myself, would still be at the head office twenty-four years later.

Henry Svazas, now Senior Vice-President of Development, in charge of real estate, is that other man. He first met Ron while trying to sell him a store site for a new Tim Hortons location. He was so good at negotiating the deal for his client that Ron wanted him working for his own company instead. Over the years, Henry has been responsible for the majority of Tim Hortons land deals throughout the country, and he is now assisted by a staff of more than fifteen. Henry's quick mind always seemed to be slightly ahead of his physical actions. Although he was highly skilled in sports, he never seemed to have everything together as he arrived at the office or left it. He always seemed to be carrying open brief-cases stuffed with wads of paper. He never walked; he dogtrotted

Bill Moir, Ron Joyce, me, and Paul House at the Ontario store owners' regional meeting, Harbour Castle Hotel, Toronto, November 28, 2001. Bill, Ron, and Paul are presenting me with a soapstone carving. BOB CHAMBERS

to and from the parking lot. His steering wheel was his desk, and he spread out maps and deeds on the front seat of his car to help him fulfill the real estate broker's three requirements — location, location, and location — for Tim Hortons.

When the meeting was over, I waited while the executive members conferred amongst themselves. After about fifteen minutes, Ron came up the stairs to meet me, put out his hand, and said, "Welcome to Tim Hortons." That was it. One month later, I was the new Tim Hortons advertising manager.

Working with the Black family and learning from their entrepreneurial skills would prove priceless in my career with Tim Hortons. Black's knew their market and could take a risk, knowing that there are only *three* things in life you can count on: death, taxes, and *change*. If they didn't try, their business wouldn't grow. I learned not only to expect changing circumstances, but, for better or for worse, to anticipate that customers, too, would change. From Black's launch of the four-inch print, I learned the value of intense store staff training before the event. Finally, Eddie Black, Sr. had told me, "Ron, you can't sell apples from an empty barrel." He meant that a retail business must have lots of stock on and under the shelf. I would find that precept equally important in the food business. No matter how fresh the donuts, no one wants to buy the last one on the tray.

To this day, if you look into any of the old company records, you will find no letter of employment referring to me, and no contracts. A simple handshake expressed the faith I had quickly gained in Ron Joyce. In fact, in the early days, a handshake often was the most important part of agreements made, not just with employees, but between new store owners and Ron Joyce and Tim Horton. I didn't know it then, but I had just committed myself to grabbing the tail of a comet. It would be a twenty-four-year ride filled with a lot of emotions, one of which would never be boredom.

Tim Horton showing off a donut in the late 1960s. TDL

CHAPTER TWO

In the Beginning
Who Put the Dough in the Donuts?

1 HOCKEY PLAYER
1 FAVOURITE BARBER SHOP
1 FORMER DRUMMER
1 POLICE OFFICER

This would prove to be the ideal recipe to bake up one of Canada's most successful restaurant chains: Tim Horton Donuts. Here are the highlights and a clarification.

First, the true Tim Hortons aficionado may question which company name is correct: Horton, Horton's, or Hortons. They are, in fact, all correct, or have been at one time or another. When the company started in 1964, the name was Tim Horton Donuts, referring directly to the name of the co-founder, Tim Horton. There was one key product line at the time, donuts. Coffee was so strongly associated with donuts that they were almost one product.

As the years progressed and the product line expanded, the name was commonly written "Horton's" when referring to products such as sandwiches, cakes, cookies, and of course coffee and donuts. Everything from business cards to outside pylon signs then read "Tim Horton's," without specific reference to any product. The name itself was developing into a strong national brand.

About 1992, the name was legally changed to "Hortons," since it stood now for a company as a brand unto itself. Further, that's how people most commonly referred to the company: "Meet me at Tim Hortons," not "Meet me at Tim Horton's donuts." The name was changed to suit the changing times and the changing customer base. In addition, the expansion into Quebec was respected, taking into consideration that in French, there are no possessive nouns.

In the beginning, there was the hockey player, Miles Gilbert (Tim) Horton, born January 12, 1930, in Cochrane, Ontario. Although the Great Depression had made life miserable for his family, he started skating and playing hockey at the age of five. As he got older, he aimed for a professional career in hockey as his means to pull himself out of poverty. By 1952, he was a star defenseman with the Toronto Maple Leafs.

According to Lori, his wife, Tim had acquired a love for donuts between 1949 and 1952, while he was playing for the Pittsburgh Hornets, the Toronto Maple Leafs farm team. He had particularly admired a certain donut shop. The owners made great donuts, and the success of their twenty-four-hour-a-day business was obvious. Tim was always concerned about what he would do after he retired from hockey. Even the biggest stars earned comparatively small salaries, especially compared with today's multi-million-dollar deals. He needed a post-hockey career, a business that would guarantee financial security for him and his family. Knowing that the Hannigan brothers, who were also with the Leaf organization, had made a go of it outside the world of hockey in the restaurant business, Tim believed that the restaurant trade would be the place to invest his retirement time and money.

Next, the barber shop. In the early 1960s, Tim liked to get his traditional brush cut at a particular neighbourhood barber shop called Benny's, which was in the Colony Plaza at Lawrence and Warden avenues, Scarborough. Beside the barber shop was Your Do-Nut Shop, owned and run by a gentleman named Jim Charade. Because of the taste and passion for donuts Tim had acquired in Pittsburgh, he was naturally attracted to this little shop. It was not unique in the Toronto area, but it captured his attention because of its proximity to his favourite barber shop.

The man who introduced Tim Horton to Jim Charade was Dennis Griggs. Dennis, born in 1938, was sixteen years old when he first met Tim in 1954. They were both coaching in a baseball league. By 1963, Dennis had a company called VIP, which made the signage and promotional items for Jim Charade's Your Do-Nut Shop, and Dennis ended up managing the shop for Jim. It was Dennis who provided the shy Toronto Maple Leaf defenseman with his initial business introduction to Jim and his entrée into the donut business.

A former drummer, Jim Charade had found playing drums for a living financially precarious, to say the least. Born in Quebec in 1934, Jim came to Toronto in 1952, at the age of eighteen, to seek fame and fortune. When Jim's brother Paul realized that Jim was looking for something a little more stable than playing drums for a living, Paul passed on some news: the Vachon Cake Company, the Quebec manufacturer of Joe Louis sweet cakes and other bakery

In 1989, Jim Charade, Ron Joyce, and Robert Morrow, the mayor of Hamilton, celebrate the twenty-fifth anniversary of Tim Hortons at the location of the first store, 65 Ottawa Street, Hamilton. COURTESY OF JIM CHARADE

products, wanted to expand into the Ontario market. They needed a Toronto representative. Although the Vachons were good bakers running a successful business, they needed a bilingual sales rep. Jim was totally bilingual, but he had no knowledge of the baking business.

Jim Charade joined the Vachon organization in 1955, and soon he discovered that Joe Louis cakes and other Vachon products were a tough sell. According to Jim, the cakes were produced with extra sugars and sweeteners, not only to appeal to the famous Quebec sweet tooth, but also to give them a long supermarket shelf life. Unfortunately, Ontarians did not have as strong a taste for these ultra-sweet treats at that time.

Jim encouraged the Vachon people to develop a donut plant in

Ontario to accommodate local preferences. They listened, and Jim began to operate the new Vachon plant and deliver these locally produced fresh donuts to the Vachon wholesale accounts. Then Jim had the idea of opening a donut shop and selling the product directly to the consumer. The Vachon group did not fully agree with operating a store directly under their own name, fearing that doing so would disturb their wholesale trade.

In February, 1962, Jim finally struck an agreement with Vachon: he could open up his own donut shop and still remain their employee. John Lynn, who would later be hired by Tim Hortons, was a key person in helping Jim to set up this independent outlet. Jim liked the name of the Buffalo, New York, restaurants called Your Host, and he simply modified the name for his own establishment: Your Do-Nut Shop. Jim produced his donuts fresh in the store, and soon he had achieved such success that he could not keep his full-time job running the Vachon donut plant. In the fall, he resigned from Vachon and devoted all his time to running Your Do-Nut Shop.

Tim Horton began to frequent Jim's donut shop, and Jim and his manager, Dennis Griggs, both felt that the name and the fame of Tim Horton would attract customers if Tim joined the business. Tim loved donuts, but the idea of developing a successful business solely around the sale of donuts and tea or coffee was truly unusual, particularly in Canada. Tim was more interested in restaurants, particularly those that sold familiar foods like hamburgers and chicken, although he could see adding donuts to the menu.

Tim liked the fast pace at which Jim and Dennis operated their business, so he agreed to join them. Jim Charade became president and Tim Horton vice-president of their new company, Jimantim Ltd., which opened a total of five chicken and hamburger eateries called Tim Horton Restaurants, one of them on Yonge Street in downtown Toronto, next to A&A records and Sam the Record Man. However, the chicken and hamburger chain struggled financially.

Gerry and Oakley Horton's hamburger restaurant in North Bay, Ontario. COURTESY OF JERI-LYNN HORTON JOYCE

There was a lot of competition in the business, and apparently Tim Horton's name did not carry enough weight to change people's established hamburger and chicken eating habits.

Tim Horton was quiet man and rather shy with his adoring fans. He would never turn aside an autograph hunter, but he found it hard to stay in the limelight long enough for the fans to collect his signature. This personality trait meant that he was a bit reluctant to support the restaurants with personal appearances, and so they couldn't get the full benefit of his fame. He became even less available at the height of the hockey season. Meanwhile, the little Your Do-Nut Shop grew so successful that, according to Jim Charade, it supported the restaurants.

A different hamburger restaurant opened in North Bay, Ontario, in 1964. According to Tim's daughter, Jeri-Lynn Horton Joyce, her dad financed the operation, but her Uncle Gerry (after whom she was named) and her grandfather, Oakley Horton, ran it. They offered "Charcoal broiled Hamburgs and hot dogs," and the pole sign in front of the chalet-style building featured the number 7 — Tim's jersey number — in the outline of a maple leaf above the restaurant's name: Tim Horton Charcoal Broiled Hamburgers. Jim Charade said that, although he helped to open the restaurant amongst a swarm of shad flies, he was not a partner in this restaurant. Because it was adjacent to Gerry and Oakley's Shell service station, and their used car dealership was on the other side of the service station, customers always found parking easy. Although strictly speaking this store was not part of the Jimantim chain, it taught the owners the importance of having plenty of parking in front of the store, knowledge that Tim would put to work in the near future.

Jim Charade wanted to expand the donut business, but the other stores they opened in Toronto were unprofitable. Overwhelming competition from other food businesses, such as Harvey's and McDonald's, combined with lack of parking space at the downtown Tim Horton's restaurants, contributed to the lacklustre performance. In addition, staffing and supervising the outlets twenty-four hours a day, seven days a week proved difficult, and training this staff to produce fresh product every day became even harder. However, the success of the first store in the Colony Plaza made Jim, Dennis, and Tim believers in the donut shop concept, and they all knew that this setup had succeeded in the United States. Through 1963, they continued to explore opportunities to expand in the Toronto market, but their real discovery turned out to be a service station for sale on Ottawa Street in Hamilton; the owner had offered to "build to suit." The deal was struck, and the former gas station became the first Tim Horton Donut Shop.

Tim, Dennis, and Jim realized that Hamilton, a good, solid working man's city, would be a choice location for their fledgling donut business. At the time, going into a restaurant and buying only a cup of tea or coffee and a fresh donut was a novelty in

The first Tim Horton's Donuts, 65 Ottawa Street, Hamilton, Ontario, as it appeared in the spring of 1979. The photo was taken about two weeks before this original building was torn down and replaced by a modern Tim Hortons store. RB

Hamilton; there appeared to be only one other donut shop, which operated on Main Street. They recognized that a shop that stayed open twenty-four hours a day, every day, would attract steel workers coming off shift, hungry and thirsty for a fresh donut with — in those days — their tea. Unlike supermarket donuts, the Tim Horton donut was made to be eaten within hours, not days. At least twice every twenty-four hours, coinciding with the steel workers' shift changes, hot, fresh donuts emerged from the Tim Hortons kitchen. Although, according to Dennis Griggs, this little donut shop lost money on more than one occasion, it soon became the flagship of a successful new business.

As the men soon discovered, running a successful business in Hamilton and other restaurants in Toronto made for a tough commute, and they found controlling the business difficult. Largely for this reason, they eventually closed Your Do-Nut Shop so they could concentrate their energy on the success of the Hamilton store.

The business and personal relationship between Jim Charade and Tim Horton remained strong through all the ups and downs of startup. Jim told me that Tim was truly his best friend. But it would take one more person to make a single donut shop a booming success and eventually a national chain, and that person was Ronald Vaughn Joyce.

Ron Joyce was born on October 19, 1930, in Tatamagouche, Nova Scotia. Four years later, his father, Willard Joyce, was killed in an accident. Grace Jollymore Joyce, then twenty-three, was left to raise Ron, four, his brother Willard (Bill), two, and their soon-to-be born sister, Gwenythe (Gwen). It was no easy task; in the depths of the Great Depression, even putting food on the table presented a huge challenge. As a youngster, Ron did more than his share by working at the Tatamagouche creamery and a fruit processing plant, as well as going to school until he completed grade ten. In the spring of 1947, he moved to Hamilton, Ontario, with little more than the change in his pocket to seek greater fortune. First he found a job with the American Can Company, and then he worked for Firestone. In 1951 he joined the Canadian Navy, and when he returned to Hamilton in 1956, he joined the Hamilton Police Force. Now with a wife and four children to support, he had to "moonlight" to supplement his pay cheque, which, in the early 1960s, was less than $100 a week. While working as a police officer, he drove a banana delivery truck, and he also drove for Brinks Security. In 1963, he purchased a Dairy Queen franchise, and once he got a taste of what he called "selling fun," he never looked back. Dairy Queen turned down his efforts to buy more franchises because he had insufficient financial backing, a big mistake for Dairy Queen but a lucky break for Ron Joyce and a bonanza for the fast food industry of North America.

In his travels on his police motorcycle, Ron had often stopped in at the first Tim Horton donut shop on Ottawa Street, and he

Ron Joyce and Tim Horton, about 1968. TDL

had seen the success of that store and the potential for future growth. When he first got to know Jim Charade and Dennis Griggs, he had not yet met Tim Horton. Jim Charade was having problems with the Tim Horton restaurants in Toronto, he did not like commuting to Hamilton, and, to tell the truth, he did not really like making donuts. Further, he needed money to reduce the debt load created by the restaurants. Tim Horton, on his part, kept a gruelling schedule as a star defenseman with the Toronto Maple Leafs, and he realized that he needed help to keep his share of the successful donut shop going strong.

Ron Joyce provided the solution to their problems. Ron borrowed money and cashed in everything he could to buy out Jim Charade's for $10,000, a princely sum in those days. Thus, on May 17, 1964, he became the first franchisee of store #1, the converted gas station on Ottawa Street in Hamilton, under the newly registered corporate name Tim Donut Ltd. Jim remained available to help as the new company got its start. Later, Ron often said, "In the first year with store #1 on Ottawa Street in Hamilton, Ontario, [Tim and I] did $50,000. We thought it was phenomenal. I had no idea just how far we were going to go."

Today, the franchise fee is $50,000, and the total investment is between $350,00 and $450,000 depending upon the size and location of the store. This fee includes seven weeks of training at the head office in Oakville, Ontario, a finished store ready to go into operation, and the support of the TDL staff to get the new business off to a good start. In Ron Joyce's case, some of the meagre assistance he received proved less than beneficial. His trial-and-error method of learning how to run a Tim Hortons franchise helped him and Tim to train new store owners for success as they increased the number of stores.

Ron loved the donut business. He liked to see the happiness a donut and a hot drink would bring to a customer, a far cry from the policeman's reality of giving out parking tickets and locking up drunks. Ron also had a bottomless pool of strength, intelligence, and energy. Where Jim Charade believed initially that a "star" name brought business, Ron ascribed success to Tim Horton's solid, steady-as-you-go attitude plus a very sound food product. Tim's warm personality and his name certainly drew attention to the donut shops, but Tim himself was rather shy. Although he loved hockey, he was not comfortable with the fame it brought him. Both he and Ron believed that the quality of the product and the service would bring customers back again and again. This belief proved to be the keystone of the company's success.

Ron began to look for new donut ideas and an expert in the baking field to develop them. He found what he was looking for in John Lynn. John had helped Jim Charade get started in the donut business, both in the introduction of donuts as a Vachon product and in establishing Jim's own Your Do-Nut Shop. John looked just like everyone's mental image of a baker: five-foot-nine, black hair, and dark rimmed glasses, with an irrepressible spirit and a booming voice and laugh. Even though he eventually held the position of General Manager of Operations at Tim Donut Ltd., his first love was and remains baking,

In the late 1950s, when Jim Charade started in the donut business, a company called the Joe Lowe Corporation (better known in the trade as "Jo-Lo") supplied mixes and equipment to the Vachon plant and his shop. John Lynn worked for Jo-Lo. He always seemed to be on call when Jim had a baking or production problem, and he helped Jim through the opening of Your Do-Nut Shop and continued with the opening of Tim Horton Donuts in Hamilton. When Jo-Lo merged with Robin Hood, John left his long-standing position and joined TDL. He made the change, he says, for two reasons: he enjoyed working with a small company, as Tim Hortons then was, and he was swayed by Ron Joyce, who convinced him that he could fill a void at the fledgling company. John started with Tim Donut Ltd. in July, 1974, when he and another new owner, Gary O'Neill, opened store #43 in Moncton, New Brunswick. John stayed with the company for seventeen years, working from the head office in Oakville, and he retired in 1991.

John was not alone in the baking department. In 1969, when there were only a dozen stores in the chain, Jim Flemming joined Tim Hortons. Jim was truly a hands-on production man. He, too, stayed with Tim Hortons for over twenty-five years, working mainly as District Manager and overseeing the opening of stores throughout the country. One of the major differences between John and Jim was that John was good at letting others watch him work. In fact, in the early 1980s, John Lynn appeared in a television commercial as a baker, carrying out a fresh tray of Tim

Hortons Strawberry Timtarts. Jim, on the other hand, could produce baked goods with the best of them, just as long as no one tried to point a camera at him or got in his way in the kitchen.

It's interesting to look back and note that Tim Hortons began with the classic depression-driven formula for success. The founders were used to long, irregular hours and working through holidays as need be in the entertainment business, professional sports, or law enforcement. They started with no support other than their own ability, ambition, and willingness to work hard. At first, the company had little money and no capital, and there were no recipes, production formulas, or business patterns to follow.

Innovation has always been another key part of the Tim Hortons success story. In the early days, serving fresh donuts was a novelty, and so was twenty-four-hour-a-day operation. New kinds of donuts, such as the Apple Fritter, maintained the novelty. Ron Joyce himself is credited with the Chocolate Walnut Crunch, and he and John Lynn developed the Raisin Dutchie after John got all the information he could from the California raisin board.

Initially, the Tim Hortons marketing plan was simple: a famous co-founder who was a member of a hockey team that was winning Stanley Cups. His name appeared on the store fronts. Owners would announce that Tim Horton, star defenseman for the Toronto Maple Leafs, and his teammates would appear at the grand opening of their new Tim Hortons store. They would load the shelves with fresh donuts, stand back, and watch the people come streaming in. The company was starting to roll.

The interior of a Tim Hortons store, about 1982. TDL

CHAPTER THREE

"We Were All Like Family"

AS I INTERVIEWED PEOPLE for *Tales from Under the Rim*, one phrase kept popping up: "When Tim Hortons was starting, we were just like a big family. We helped each other out. We shared our problems and our successes." This spirit lives today, but in the beginning this closeness was about all they had to keep them going. People like John Lynn and Jim Flemming became part of the store owners' lives by helping them to get their stores running successfully, and some families became part of Tim Hortons.

One such family is the Mattatalls, whose history with the company is in its third generation. Eddie Mattatall, one of the first franchisees, started with little more than sheer faith in a brand new company. His story begins in 1930, when, at the age of three months, he moved permanently from Boston, Massachusetts, to Tatamagouche, Nova Scotia, where he lived with his grandparents. He grew up there with another Tatamagouche native, Ron Joyce.

In 1947, when he was seventeen, Eddie "went down the road" to Hamilton. He had heard from his friend Ron, who had moved there six months earlier, that jobs were far more plentiful in Hamilton than in rural Nova Scotia. Eddie took a job with the American Can Company and spent more than eighteen years there. He met Florence, they got married, and in 1951, they shared a house with Ron and his first wife, Linda. This house-sharing didn't last long. In 1951, Ron decided to join the Navy, and Ed and Florence found the house too expensive to keep by themselves. Ed still worked for American Can when Ron came back to Hamilton in 1956 and joined the police force, but the men kept in touch. Like Ron, Ed hoped that someday he would have a business of his own. In those days, a lot of people dreamed of owning a hamburger franchise, and Ed and another friend, Al Murray, tried to get a Red Barn outlet. Fortunately for both men and for TDL, their efforts failed. Ron had often imagined with Ed the great business deals they could do, and soon after Ron bought into the Tim Horton Donut Shop on Ottawa Street, Ed could see that this new company was enjoying great success. Ron wanted Ed to purchase the franchise of the second store, on Concession Street, but for one reason and another, Ed got cold feet and didn't take Ron's advice. He remembers, too, that his reluctance had a lot to do with not having enough money.

The Concession Street franchise was bought by a man who had been a baker at Ron's store, Casey Weilhower, who became the second franchisee in the TDL system, after Ron Joyce. According to Jim Charade, the very first person to operate the Tim Horton Donut Shop for him and Tim was Spencer Brown, but at that time, the TDL name had not been registered. The name was registered at the same time that Ron Joyce started, and thus Joyce was the first official franchisee of Tim Horton Donuts operated by TDL.

Now Eddie Mattatall saw the success of two Tim Hortons stores. After kicking himself for not taking that second store, he pushed hard to purchase the next franchise that Tim Hortons had to offer. On April 3, 1967, Ed became the third franchisee in the system, purchasing store #1 on Ottawa Street in Hamilton for $24,000. Ron Joyce had decided to sell his store to concentrate with Tim on the franchise expansion of the company, rather than running one or more of the donut shops. Getting new franchisees was not an easy task in the early days, so Ron allowed Ed to pay him $9,000 down and make payments of $400 a month; Ron carried the balance of the loan.

Ron spent just two weeks teaching Ed to bake before he was on his own. The training program was very practical, with Ron teaching Eddie at the Ottawa Street location. Learning the donut business, Tim Hortons style, continued in this seat-of-the-pants fashion until store #66 in the chain, the twelfth store in Hamilton, opened for business on February 25, 1977; the official ribbon cutting took place on April 6. Although it looked like and functioned as a regular store, it had a full training facility in the basement. New store owners would now receive practical, hands-on training, plus lectures and lessons in administration, in a program that would range from seven to nine weeks.

It had taken thirteen years and sixty-six stores to get a full training facility, "Donut U," under way; the facility served the chain for the next nine years. In 1985, store #66 remained in operation, but the training facility moved from its basement to Oakville, becoming part of store #250 on Wyecroft Road. By 1992, this Oakville store became part of the TDL head office, and store #250 relocated across the road to an even larger facility and training complex. Now, all new franchisees in Canada and the United States are trained in this building. The attached, fully operational store remains an important facet of the training program, allowing the senior trainees to gain actual experience in an active store before taking on the responsibility of running their own stores.

Eddie Mattatall said that Ron convinced him to walk away

from eighteen and a half years of seniority with the American Can Company during a quick profit-and-loss view of store #1 at the Glendale Golf Club. Ron scribbled out the details on a paper napkin over lunch; Ed recalls Ron saying, "Well, the store is doing this, it will cost you this and this, and it should make something like this." That was it. The numbers, his total faith in his lifelong friend, and his observation of the success of the two stores induced Ed Mattatall change careers. He earned enough at American Can, but, he said, in the first nine months at Tim Hortons, he made $17,000 and felt like a millionaire. Florence agreed, but added that the reason they felt so rich was that they couldn't get out of the store to spend their money.

Just fourteen months after acquiring their first store, Eddie and Florence opened a third location, store #7 in the chain. Located in Stoney Creek, it would not prove to be an instant home run. When it opened in June, 1968, it had very limited parking, and cars could barely turn around in the lot. Start-up was difficult, but this Hamilton location eventually did become a success, just like the Mattatalls' first two stores.

Another of the first franchisees, Eldon Fawcett, was working for Westinghouse in Hamilton when he became interested in Tim Horton Donut Shops. He came into the system in 1967, in the same year as Ed Mattatall. Eldon believed that his job at Westinghouse would be taken over by a computer. He didn't know Ron or Tim personally, but he had watched the first three donut shops go into operation. The fourth shop, on King Street West, was being built. He kept calling Ron Joyce to set up an appointment to discuss becoming a store owner. Finally, Ron set up a meeting that included Tim as well as Eldon and himself to discuss the business over lunch. Once again, Joyce wrote out profit-and-loss estimates on a Tim Hortons napkin.

This style of financial reporting nonplussed Eldon, and he told Ron and Tim that he wanted a some first-hand information before consummating a deal. To best answer Eldon's queries, Ron and Tim sent him to speak with Ed Mattatall. Eldon told Ed about his uneasiness with the estimates scribbled on a napkin, but Eddie put Eldon's mind at ease. That was all he had had to go by, Eddie told him, and his own belief in Ron and Tim and the Hortons donut and coffee shops was all paying off. Eldon bought the fifth store in the chain, on Plains Road in Burlington, Ontario.

Eldon was earning around $7,000 a year at Westinghouse. In his first year of running the donut shop, he made $27,000, with an initial investment of around $35,000. Like Eddie Mattatall, Eldon Fawcett started from napkin-style accounting, worked night and day, and quickly succeeded. This pattern was characteristic of the early members of the franchise chain. The franchisees proved again and again that, with Tim Hortons, good luck and good fortune were the outcome of hard work.

In spite of their casual approach to explaining the company's finances to prospective franchisees and their inclination to do business on a handshake, Ron and Tim's original agreement with Eldon Fawcett was about three pages in length — short by today's standards, but as businesslike as was needed at that time. Florence Mattatall says that a few years later, when the store owners began to purchase flours, mixes, and coffee directly from TDL, invoicing was Tim's responsibility. She always knew when Tim was on a hockey road trip: the invoicing would come to a sudden stop until he returned.

In the late 1960s, the sophistication of the modern Tim Hortons warehouse system was well in the future. This warehouse system would be designed to purchase and distribute the Tim Hortons raw materials through huge volume discounts passed on to the franchisees. When Eddie Mattatall started, he had to buy his flour and mixes directly from Jo-Lo, and thus another new franchisee got to know the skills of John Lynn, who still worked at Jo-Lo. To save money, Ed even bought his own truck so he could pick up his supplies directly.

The second generation of Mattatalls started in the Tim Hortons donut business at the same time as the first generation. In 1967, at the age of sixteen, Miles Mattatall learned baking at his father's side. It would become Miles's weekend job as he went through school. In 1975, he joined the company officially by buying into one of his father's stores. Now he owns fourteen stores in the Hamilton area. The third generation, Miles's son Chris, has become Director of Operations; he oversees all of Miles Mattatall's stores. Ryan, who is two years younger than Chris, also intends to pursue a career with TDL.

The Mattatalls relate stories that demonstrate the feeling customers often have that they're part of the Tim Hortons family. Many take "their" store very much to heart. Sometimes they take matters into their own hands. For instance, Miles had difficulty with a particular Hamilton police officer, who took it upon himself to step behind the counter during the night shift and not only pour his own coffee but also to make a fresh pot. For reasons of safety, sanitation, and store security, customers are absolutely not allowed behind the counter, no matter who they might be. Miles barred the officer from the store. Soon the police department held internal meetings and established a series of "can and cannot" rules concerning behaviour in Tim Hortons stores. After the offending officer apologized profusely, Miles allowed him to come back into his store, but he never went behind the counter again.

Tim Hortons started out in Hamilton, that's where the business first flourished, and the greater Hamilton area is still the easiest place in the country to find a Tim Hortons store. With a total population of 450,000 and approximately eighty stores, Hamilton has the largest number of stores for one city and its immediate suburbs. However, its average of one store for every 5,600 people doesn't come close to the average of Moncton, New Brunswick. With its suburbs, Moncton boasts a population of 100,000, served by thirty-five stores: approximately one store for every 2,900 people. Gary O'Neill owns all thirty-five stores.

Like Ron Joyce and Eddie Mattatall, Gary O'Neill also hails from Tatamagouche, Nova Scotia. Also like Ron and Eddie, he moved to Hamilton by himself as a teenager to seek better employment. During his teens and twenties, he worked at several of Hamilton's large manufacturing companies, including Westinghouse and Stelco, and in due course he met and married Mary, who was also from Nova Scotia. At the age of twenty-eight, Gary inquired about getting into the Tim Hortons business. Gary had been a customer of the Upper James Street store, he observed its success, and he began to think that, with a wife and family, he should be looking at running his own business. He and Mary had thought about moving back to the Maritimes. In 1974, Gary first met Ron Joyce to ask him about establishing a franchise in Moncton. Once again, Ron supported the new business, in this case by helping Gary get the bank loan he needed; Gary believes that this franchise cost about $45,000. He opened the first store outside Ontario, #43, on July 17, 1974.

Gary never really knew Tim Horton except for the few times he found Tim helping out in the Oakville warehouse. Tim, he said, had arms like tree trunks, and he seemed to take great delight in personally loading huge bags of flour to fulfill store orders. However, Gary did become well acquainted with John Lynn, who would also gain great respect within the Tim Hortons chain. He was trained by John, who had just joined the company, and Gary's Moncton store opening was the first John had ever attended.

Starting a Tim Hortons in Moncton was not easy. The first winter was terrible, with a lot of snow. Business was so bad that

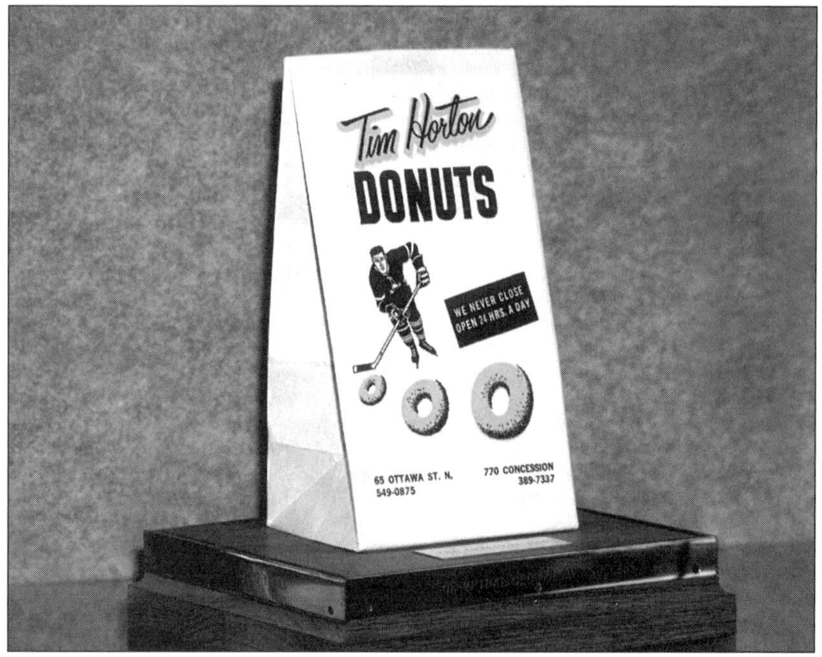

An original donut bag, about 1965, showing the addresses of the only two stores operating at that time. The three donuts represent the three oldest of Tim's four daughters, Jeri-Lynn, Kim, Kelly, and Traci. This bag is on display at the TDL head office. RB

Gary could not even pay his apartment rent for three months. In spite of everything, though, the business succeeded, and Gary opened his second store on the other side of Moncton four years later, in August, 1978.

Donuts were the big seller in Moncton. At that time, Gary said, he was lucky to sell a case of coffee a week — that's only about 1,000 eight-ounce cups, or six cups per hour. Tea and coffee sold about equally for the first couple of years, perhaps because Maritimers were inveterate tea-drinkers, but coffee's popularity increased because it's is easier to handle as a take-out beverage. Gary had the first drive through window in the Tim Hortons system in the late 1980s. Ron Joyce was very concerned with drive-throughs, Gary says, because he believed that stores would lose impulse sales. People using the drive-through window couldn't come into the store for coffee and perhaps one treat and then find themselves yielding to the temptation of a beautiful display of other products. This was certainly true, but Gary pointed out that other companies sold coffee and food through drive-through windows, and Tim Hortons should not be left out of those sales. Gary believed that, if he had a drive-through, a mother taking kids to school, for instance, or someone who didn't want to take the extra time to park and come into the store would become customers. He also knew that a single Tim Hortons owner had to try it, and he wanted to be the first. The drive-through became part of his first store, #43. After just two months, the overall sales of the store showed a noticeable increase because of the drive-through.

In 1992, Tim Hortons would take the popular drive-through idea into many of the stores, and location #645, built in Oakville, tested a more advanced version of the concept: the first "Double Drive Thru" (spelled "thru" on the signage because this abbreviation uses less space than "through" and is just as easy to understand). This feature allowed customers to approach the service windows from either the driver's or the passenger's side. TDL opened this Double Drive Thru near head office to get a clear understanding of how many customers would use the passenger-side window. This research would tell store owners whose location would allow only passenger-window access what kind of business they could expect, compared to the business achieved by driver-window access. True to form, TDL did not want to see a store owner invest money in a new concept, a passenger-side-only drive-through window, without first getting reliable sales figures.

The experiment succeeded, demonstrating that passenger-window drive-through delivery could be profitable, and this style of drive-through became popular with many store owners across Canada. Donuts, muffins, bagels, and other baked products are delivered from the main store to the "DDT" location, and beverages are produced at the site. Because installing one of these units requires a very small amount of real estate, store owners can increase their market presence even where land is either scarce or very costly.

Gary O'Neill tried out the DDT concept with great success. But, he says, in his case, because of the amount of land he had available, both windows could have driver-window access, since traffic could enter from two different streets. Once again, Gary had taken someone else's idea and run with it in his own unique way.

At least once a year, it seems, customers try to make a Tim Hortons store a drive-through of their own accord by literally driving through one of the outside walls. No one has done it on purpose that I know of, and I don't remember any serious injuries associated with customers accelerating instead of braking, reversing instead of driving forward, or leaving their vehicle in "drive" instead of "park."

CHAPTER FOUR

Going Coast to Coast

ONE MONTH AFTER GARY O'NEILL went into business in Moncton, Willard (Bill) Joyce, Ron's brother, opened the second franchise in the Maritimes store #44, on Wyse Road, Dartmouth, Nova Scotia. Jim Flemming, the patient baker, attended the open-ing of this store. Today, Jim's key chain bears a small, well-worn brass tag. The inscription on one side reads:

Tim Horton Donuts
Halifax
October 25/75
Jim Flemming

The inscription on the other side says:

Boys oh boys, that's some good!

Bill Joyce gave Jim this tag at the opening of his second store, #53, on Herring Cove Road, Halifax. Bill opened this store fifteen months after starting his first location in Dartmouth, kept it for a period of time, and then sold it to the current franchisees, Sandy and Beverley Shearer.

Bill was two years younger than Ron. Famous as Ron is for his parties, and for making sure everyone around him knows that, when it's time to party, you party hard, I sometimes believed it was Bill who taught his older brother these skills. More than once I had the pleasure of enjoying a dinner with Bill. He would reminisce about his childhood days and tell me how they made him appreciate the life he was currently enjoying. Even eating a lobster brought memories of his youth: lobsters, he said, had been a constant mainstay of their diet and not an expensive treat. Giving someone a memento like that small key chain tag engraved with one of his favourite down-east phrases was typical of Bill. Years later, he would pass out little pins that exemplified a Maritimer's love of life. He *lived* every day of his sixty-five years, passing away in 1997.

Eight more stores would open in the Maritimes and twenty-one more in Ontario before the first Quebec store opened, #72, in Rosemere on July 23, 1977. In the next three years, Tim Hortons opened fifty-three more stores, including two in Newfoundland and our first western locations. Only then did we expand further into Quebec, with store #125 in Boucherville and #127 in Sept-Îles.

It was Ron Joyce who pushed to enter the Quebec market and increase the number of stores there. With its huge population, it could not be bypassed. Because of the family-style culture of Tim Hortons, it was important for the franchisees to be local people, as much as possible. In the beginning, some Quebec franchisees came from central Canada, but in the long run, getting local owners was the best plan. Quebec, with its very well-known sweet tooth, made an excellent market, and over the years, the original thinking for new products has often come out of Quebec. Store owners there were the first to think their customers would like to buy soup. They tried it, found it a great success, and eventually first soup and then sandwiches were introduced chain-wide. Innovative thinking was just one of the many advantages the company gained from the Quebec stores.

From a marketing point of view, the three-year delay between the opening of the Rosemere store and the Boucherville and Sept-Îles stores proved costly and difficult. It was important to support our Quebec outlets with as much efficient marketing as we could, even when there was only a handful of stores. However, when we had only one, two, or three widely spread stores, this was not an easy task, especially considering that we also had to make sure the advertising was suitable to French tastes. Point-of-purchase advertising materials, like our radio and television commercials, were all produced by Tim Hortons for Tim Hortons. At first, we placed the copy at the bottom of the shot on our point of purchase material so it could be converted from English to French easily and at a reasonable cost, without the need to shoot everything twice. However, when I found competitors taking our discarded posters, cutting the copy off the bottom, and reusing them, we made sure our photographs included the logo, packaging, cups, or bowls. We learned to set the copy in black type only, allowing an efficient one-plate copy change from English to French. Now, with well over 150 stores in the province, Tim Hortons produces print advertising and radio and television commercials exclusively for Quebec.

At the time, I did not really understand why Ron Joyce would put a single store, or a very few stores, off by themselves in the West, the Maritimes, or Quebec, far away from the central Hamilton core. In 1977, TDL had even opened two stores in St. John's, Newfoundland, which seemed to some of the Oakville staff to be about as far away as stores could get. The media support rippling out from central Canada simply couldn't reach that far without making additional media buys on either local stations or via the television networks. After talking in detail with people like Eddie Mattatall in Hamilton, Gary O'Neill in Moncton, and Art Jenkins, whose St. Albert, Alberta, store was one of the early Western franchises, I realized that each store or group of stores had to prove itself locally and with the immediate market before it could expand to the larger surrounding population via the media. Except for the few early stores that could trade on Tim Horton's name as a hockey superstar, the Tim Horton Donut Shops had to prove they were a viable part of the community by building a good, strong local clientele. Ron had learned this himself, and he was prepared to help in the initial struggle of a new franchisee in a new area, where the product and the name were not as commonly known as they were in central Canada. Today, because of the size of the chain, it's possible to offer new territories media support that "borrows" advertising dollars for their immediate use, even though they may not yet be producing enough revenue themselves. In the early days, though, the marketing dollars were just not there, and franchisees had to build locally and push hard to get new territories going.

On a western trip in 1978, with Ron Joyce and Henry Svazas, Senior Vice President of real estate, I learned about a land purchase made by Tim Horton himself. We were standing on a roadside in Surrey, British Columbia, when I mentioned that a vacant corner just ahead of us would be a great spot for a Tim Hortons location. "Tim bought that land years ago," Ron said.

His remark made me wonder whether, if Tim had lived, the expansion of the company might have been more equally divided between the West and the East. Perhaps when Ron became the sole owner of the company he felt more comfortable with developing into the Maritimes first. Tim, who grew up in Northern Ontario, may have realized that Ron would want to develop the East, so he would work on western development. Finding out that Tim had bought this Surrey property reinforced my speculation. Aside from such personal factors, the population in the East is more concentrated than the population throughout the West, and travelling to the Maritimes from central Canada takes less time than travelling to the Prairies and British Columbia. Thus it may have seemed easier for the Oakville head office to work with eastern expansion.

In September, 1983, Art and Joan Jenkins became part of the Tim Hortons team with the first store in St. Albert, Alberta, store #179, and they are still with the chain today. Theirs was the fifth Tim Hortons location in western Canada. Three stores were in the Vancouver suburbs of Surrey, Langley, and Burnaby; one was by itself in Penticton, in the interior of British Columbia; and the new store #179 would also be on its own, just outside Edmonton. Art and Joan lived in Simcoe, Ontario, but both were originally from Hamilton. Art, like Eddie Mattatall, wanted to be in business for himself. Like Eddie, with his eighteen-and-a-half years at American Can Company, Art had twenty-five years of seniority at Stelco. He first became interested in Tim Hortons when he visited Ron Joyce's Ottawa Street store in Hamilton as a customer. He especially enjoyed the banana cream pies that John Lynn launched there in 1974. Ron spoke initially to Art and Joan in 1982 about buying a franchise, proposing that they go out west to St. Albert, Alberta.

Art and Joan had no idea where St. Albert was, but that didn't stop them from agreeing to go there. They discovered a community of approximately 28,000 people, a farming town that had become a bedroom community to Edmonton, a ten-minute drive down the highway. Art trained for five or six weeks at store #66, on King Street, Hamilton. One night, the store's baker didn't show up, so Art moved from the training centre kitchen to the kitchen of store #66 and did the night bake. He proved himself by rising to the challenge, and he passed his "test" bake perfectly. When he and Joan opened #179, a crew went out to the store with them for a couple of weeks to help them get rolling.

The head office stood by Art and Joan in the family spirit that is strongly woven into the Tim Hortons mentality. The store began poorly, since the only people in St. Albert who knew what a Tim Hortons location was all about were transplants from Ontario and the Maritimes. The hockey mystique seemed to have faded away, too. Everyone thought Art was Tim Horton, and he actually answered to the name! It was a nerve-racking start. Art would stand out on the highway and wonder how he could get the drivers to turn into his store. There were no big advertising dollars available, so to get sales, Art would do his regular bake every day, package a lot of the product, and drive around to various businesses, firehalls, and police stations, giving his donuts away with his business card attached. This simple strategy worked, making the community familiar with both the product and the store. Art made his rounds day after day, and he also joined the Chamber of Commerce and got involved with the Kinsmen to become known and to get the business rolling.

When the tide turned, donuts were a big seller, just as they were in the original stores when the chain began; the habit of going to Tim's for coffee had not yet started. In St. Albert, fresh donuts were a delicious novelty, and there was no direct competition for baked goods. When Art and Joan offered customers the opportunity to buy a dozen donuts and get a snack pack of Timbits free, customers lined up right out the door. Tim Hortons was the only place in town open twenty-four hours a day, seven days a week, and Art and Joan maintained the hours even though at first the night business was very sparse.

Even in the mid-1980s, Art remembers, Ron Joyce would fly out to Edmonton, come to the store, and sit on the flour bags to talk things over. A good deal of business was conducted by a handshake, just as it had been ten years earlier with Eddie Mattatall and Eldon Fawcett. As the years passed, local associations would name Art and Joan's store "business of the month" and "business of the year," and today Tim Hortons is known as a good corporate neighbour in the community. The Jenkinses now own two stores in St. Albert (the population of which has doubled) and one in Edmonton. Competition eventually came in, then failed, and Art and Joan's Tim Hortons stores are once again on their own and succeeding. Art and Joan Jenkins are just one example of the attitude and hard work ethic that has made Tim Hortons a success across the country.

Tim Hortons was expanding from coast to coast in Canada, and in 1981 we made our first venture into the United States — we opened a store in Pompano Beach, Florida. By 1983, we had opened a second Florida location in Deerfield Beach: two stores in the Sunshine State, which many Canadians call home for the winter months. The presence of so many snowbirds made that part of Florida seem like a good place to establish an American toehold, since we wouldn't have to worry about introducing two locations so far from head office. Unfortunately, our reasoning was flawed, and we learned the value of a worthy competitor. We had never faced such highly developed competition in the coffee-and-donut business before. Customers knew what to expect, but it wasn't what we offered. Many of our competitors had set a pattern of poor quality products and service, and we started with that strike against us. We had built stores in an area where a 24/7 donut and coffee operation was not the norm; the competitors closed in late afternoon. At that time, too, we could not make donuts that achieved our standards because the flour that was available was of lower quality than the flour we were used to. Although there were a lot of Canadian tourists, they certainly did not equal the number of Americans to whom the name Tim Hortons meant nothing. Also, we found the U.S. market to be highly fragmented. In Canada, a couple of media buys could cover a wide area, but in Florida, the multitude of independent radio stations and newspapers meant that our dollars had to be too finely divided. Television was far, far beyond our budget. Because of the thin market, the disreputable competition, our unusual hours, and our inadequate advertising, we decided to close the Florida stores in February, 1995.

In 1985, Tim Hortons entered the U.S. market at a closer range: Amherst and Lockport, New York, in the Buffalo area. This, too, was a tough start, with prejudice against our unsavoury competition being the hardest obstacle to overcome. The public expected a donut shop to be a shabby hangout offering poor quality products. Nothing could have been further from the Tim Hortons reality. Alec Strom, who owned stores in Fort Erie and Crystal Beach, Ontario, took on the Buffalo locations in the late 1980s. His dedicated hard work turned these operations around, making them acceptable to the American public.

Ron Joyce had predicted that the U.S. would be the next big chance for Tim Hortons, but to break into the wider American market would require time and deep pockets. Alec's Buffalo-area stores showed the way, developing a solid customer base by demonstrating the freshness and diversity of the products, the cleanliness of the stores, and the warm welcome awaiting customers every day, around the clock. The strategy this time was to fan out from the northern states and build credibility along the way, sticking at first mainly to areas where cold winters and unpredictable summers create a lifestyle much like our own, a lifestyle that is part of the fabric of Tim Hortons.

Finally, in 2002, the skills of the marketing team in Oakville and the operational teams in the U.S. paid off. The combined American operations turned the corner, showing the first-ever annual profit. Today there are over 150 stores in the northern states, including New York, Ohio, Minnesota, Massachusetts, and Michigan, and there are also stores in West Virginia and Kentucky. Aggressive expansion is planned, with targets of thirty locations per year for the next several years.

Since December, 1995, Wendy's International Inc. has owned Tim Hortons, and Canadians devoted to Tim Hortons have worried that the chain would become Americanized. This hasn't happened. The Canadian chain is bringing the Canadian product and services to the United States and actually Canadianizing American coffee. Tim Hortons is operated in the same way and with the same managerial schemes as it has for years. Astutely, Wendy's has left well enough alone, and no wonder. Although Tim Hortons has less than half as many stores as Wendy's, and although the average price of a coffee and donut is less than the average price of a hamburger and fries, Tim Hortons still accounts for 30% to 35% of Wendy's total revenues.

In the beginning, initial promotions for the openings of the stores centred around Tim Horton and his hockey buddies, plus the novelty of fresh donuts. When store #8 opened in Brantford, Ontario, on July 18, 1968, Ron Joyce and Tim Horton came with all the hockey players to sign autographs. The store offered a "grand opening special": buy a dozen donuts and get a half-dozen free.

To get the store going, John Lynn was brought in from the Jo-Lo Corporation, initially to develop and expand the pie business and increase the variety of donuts. Ron Joyce and Tim Horton rolled up their sleeves and pitched in, too. Ron and Tim produced the cake and yeast donut mixes, while John made the "small" mixes for the orange twists and special donuts. A well-scrubbed and sanitized door became his worktable because there was no room left in the kitchen — Ron and Tim had occupied it all. They worked through the night to prepare for the store opening. Around eight-thirty a.m., Ron said, he believed they had everything in good shape, so he invited everyone out for breakfast. When they got back after about an hour and a half, they had to park five blocks from the store. It was mobbed with fans wanting autographs, and they were buying donuts by the bushel. The grand opening special certainly worked. By the time they finished at ten o'clock that night, John said, "you could have taken all the donuts home in your two arms with no problem at all. We couldn't catch up."

A normal production run for a store in those days would have been approximately eighty pounds of cake and eighty pounds of yeast mix. This mix would yield about 160 to 175 dozen donuts per shift, with two shifts per day. During grand openings like the one in Brantford, the production run would be 700 pounds in twenty-four hours. That, according to John and Jim, would represent over 700 dozen donuts.

Not all openings ran smoothly, and a store's beginnings could be rough. Paul Preuss, now the owner of stores in Orangeville, Ontario, started with TDL in the summer of 1978, helping to open store #93 on Kent Street in Charlottetown, Prince Edward Island. As he acquired more stores, he found that every opening brought its own crisis and taught a new lesson in survival. When he was about to open one store, the mixer for making the donuts didn't arrive, and the store couldn't produce donuts without it. On checking, he found that the mixer had indeed left the warehouse, but it was a very heavy piece of equipment, and it had literally dropped through the floorboards of the truck carrying it. Paul and his colleagues discovered the mixer lying in a heap beside the highway. The factory rushed him a new one, and he managed to open the store on time.

At one Nova Scotia store opening, the owner ordered his baker to produce eighty pounds of yeast mix for donuts. It seems that the baker was interested in "cutting" only the equivalent of sixty pounds into actual donuts. He mixed the eighty pounds so that, if the store owner checked, he would see that the correct amount of mix had been used. Fearing that the owner would look in the garbage to see if any of the yeast mix had been discarded, the baker threw the unused twenty pounds into the trunk of his car, where it "rested" for three warm summer days. On the fourth day, the trunk exploded. So did the store owner. The baker was fired.

As in any family, the members of the Tim Hortons family didn't always get along. To Ron Joyce, the stores and the owners were like family, so if things weren't the way he wanted them, they were well advised to run for cover. All of the Tim Hortons stores had to have the same basic qualities: a clean parking lot, a lit (and, in the early days, rotating) pylon sign, capable and courteous staff providing excellent service, a clean store, and lots of great product on the shelves. The formula sounds so simple, but these standards have never been easy to maintain consistently.

Once when Ron was inspecting a store with one of the local operations supervisors, he picked up a strawberry tart, took a bite, found the quality substandard, and threw it against the nearest wall. He then picked up a cruller, took a bite, and meted out the same fate. It landed all over the same wall as the strawberry tart. He had the owner phoned and demanded his immediate presence.

When he arrived, Ron read him the riot act. A store owner who let quality slip knew no fury like that of Ronald V. Joyce, company owner. Any franchisee's toughest critics were his fellow operators and Ron Joyce himself. To run a poor store reflected badly on the other stores as well as on the sloppy owner. It brought the family down.

Ron had a quiet but volatile temper, but it was notoriously short-lived. Once, I'm told, he reprimanded two of his Nova Scotia operations staff in a car ride from Truro to Halifax. He chewed these individuals out with great gusto, but when they arrived in Halifax, he got out of the car and invited them to join him for dinner. The point had been made; it was time to move on.

Store owners ranked number one with Ron. This point was clearly brought home to me in my first year with TDL. I wrote a letter addressed to store owner Gary Wilson in Sydney, Nova Scotia, but I made the thoughtless error of not including the name of Karen, his wife, who was and is an equal partner in their business. I learned what it meant to be on Ron Joyce's wrong side very quickly. He pointed out my blunder, and I immediately sent a letter of apology and a dozen roses to Karen. She still remembers and refers somewhat fondly to my "sorry roses." It was a lesson well learned: Ron Joyce held the store owners in high esteem, and in return Ron was held in high esteem by them.

Bud Kennish was one of the earliest franchisees. Bud knew Ron Joyce from their days together on the Hamilton police force: Bud had joined in 1953, Ron in 1956. A big, strapping fellow even today, Bud looks as if he could still comfortably climb on a Harley Davidson and go on street patrol, his white hair concealed by his helmet. In those days, he and Ron would often enjoy a coffee and donut at the Tim Hortons on Ottawa Street. It stayed open all night, and the chance to stop outside the door and get a fresh hot coffee and a treat was welcome. Today, some forces discourage their members from leaving police vehicles in front of a Tim Hortons store because the picture of cops spending too much of their time drinking coffee and eating donuts has become such a cliché. Actually, it was initially one of the very few 24/7 operations that offered fresh coffee and donuts. Particularly in the wee small hours of a long shift, police officers could get a very welcome boost to help them through the night.

One time Ron and Bud rolled to a stop in front of the store. Ron asked Bud what he thought of this Tim Horton Donut Shop. Bud said it was fine. Ron asked again, "But what do you *really* think of it?" Bud reiterated his opinion, but this time Ron responded that he liked this business so much he was going to buy the place. Bud continued to frequent the shop after Ron had taken it over, and he and Ron would discuss the business. In 1965, a police constable earned about $100 a week, whereas Ron grossed over $50,000 a year from his donut shop. This persuaded Bud to cash in his police pension. In 1970, after seventeen years on the force, Bud joined Ron in the donut business, buying the franchise for store #2, on Concession Street. He owns this store today.

Bud's son had reservations about his father's career change. He was used to seeing his dad neatly attired in a police uniform. The first time he saw Bud at Tim Hortons, he was scrubbing a large pail in the kitchen. It was quite a change. Bud first met Tim when Tim was physically digging the foundations for store #4. Ron Joyce has often told this story: some school children were passing the construction sight on their way to the library with their teacher. When they saw Tim digging, one of them exclaimed, "Look, that's Tim Horton!" The teacher, obviously not a hockey fan, replied, "Yes, and if you don't keep up your school work, you'll end up digging ditches, too!"

Bud paid $35,000 for his first store. The previous franchisee had let the place slip into a shoddy condition. When Bud took it over, it had eleven stools, a cigarette machine in one corner, a jukebox in the other, and no tables. He brought in a small table from home and folding card-table chairs so people could sit down and enjoy their coffee and donut. After cleaning up the store, Bud was able to increase his production to about seventy pounds of yeast donut mix on a Monday or Tuesday and up to 130 pounds on weekends.

At about the time when Bud was getting into the business, Ron and Tim were working hard to make it grow. To save money, Ron designed the buildings on the lot layouts, and Tim ordered the equipment to fit into the store. There was essentially just one design (which I have nicknamed the "shoe box"), and store owners could reverse the design according to the demands of the building site. One time, Ron had informed Tim that the plans for a particular site had been flipped from right fixturing to left fixturing, but Tim forgot to change the order for the equipment. Every cent counted. In order to keep up with their loans for the new stores, they had to open each new location as quickly as possible so they could begin to earn income on their latest investment. For this location, their sensible plan was doomed. When the equipment arrived, it was backwards and could not be installed. Ron, whose temper was several notches higher than Tim's, was furious over his partner's mistake. Tim offered Ron one of two choices: he could go up to the top of the Burlington Skyway and jump off, or they could start again, immediately ordering the correct material and getting it in place as fast as they could.

This incident illustrates, not only the kinds of problems that could occur, but the steady, anchoring effect that Tim had on Ron. It would be a quality that Ron would soon miss forever.

The company that Tim Horton and Ron Joyce had founded in 1964 and made to flourish came to a tragic end on February 21, 1974. Tim had been playing for the Buffalo Sabres in Toronto's Maple Leaf Gardens that night against his former team, the Toronto Maple Leafs. He had driven to Toronto from Buffalo for the game in his Ford Pantera sports car, and after the game, he stopped in at the Oakville head office. Ron happened to drive by, saw Tim's car, and stopped in as well. They talked into the small hours. Tim was on painkillers for an injury that had been diagnosed as a cracked jaw, and Ron could not help but notice that he was truly suffering. He tried to convince Tim not to drive back to Buffalo, but he went anyway, leaving around three-thirty in the morning. It would be the last time that Ron would see Tim alive. Tim had a very bad reputation for driving too fast and with reckless abandon. At approximately four-thirty a.m., he passed St. Catharines policeman Mike Gula going an estimated 100 miles per hour. Gula gave chase. Near the Lake Street exit on the Q.E.W., Tim lost control of the car. It skidded off into the median, rolled several times, and came to rest in the west-bound lanes. Tim was thrown from the car and died instantly. The police found his body well over a hundred feet from the wreck. He was forty-four years old.

Ron and Tim's method of building success was to take the franchise fee collected from a new franchisees and put as much of it as they could back into the next location. They were less interested in keeping locations for themselves than in franchising them out to new owners. Retaining company stores meant paying for management teams and spending their own time on individual store operation. Instead, their plan was to increase the franchise family. Reinvesting a new franchisee's fee in the next location made the system work.

Ron and Tim had huge respect for the store owners. This would continue when Ron was building the chain after Tim's death, making sure that corporate decisions benefitted the chain as a whole.

Ron Joyce and Tim Horton lean against Tim's Alpine Tiger during the construction of store #4, at 951 King Street West, Hamilton, in 1967. TDL

Although the money was better than even Eldon Fawcett had expected, he truly earned it. He told me that it was not uncommon to get only three hours sleep a night while he was trying to get the operation of the store on an even keel. Ron and Tim had set up the system so that the lion's share of a store's profits went to the store owner. They also passed along the savings generated by the increased corporate buying power that made mass purchases of flour, coffee, other food products, and supplies attractive. TDL is built on the business of selling businesses, not on just selling franchises; the company wants the franchisees to succeed. This care for the success of individual owners, one of the strongest values of Tim Hortons, is not always present in other franchising operations. It's also true, though, that franchise companies that fail to treat owners fairly become memories in the business world.

The progress of Tim Hortons is based on making each individual franchisee successful. The success of the TDL Group Ltd. as a whole came from the growth of the operation. In the early days, fran-chisees were not deserted once their doors were opened, and they are not deserted now. The company is there to make store owners do well because the gains of the individuals bring about the growth of the chain. There has always been great emphasis on providing new product. Without new product, without listening to the fran-chisees and keeping up with the changing customer, Tim Hortons would probably have stagnated and died long ago. Ron and Tim made the stores a success through their development of product recipes and proper procedures in store operations, and the company continues to give back to the franchisees the secrets of success.

Ron Joyce has said that a franchisee coming into the business is actually buying a cash flow. It is up to the store owner to build the business and reap the savings. A store does not become an instant success. As the years pass, the profits should grow, and so should the store owner's personal equity. A successful franchisee who wants to retire from the chain has made a good living and also can sell the store to a new franchisee at its current market value.

In this way, the new franchisee has a chance to succeed and the original franchisee has made a nest egg.

The attitude of helping one another could not be better seen than at corporate conventions held at locations from Halifax to Florida and from Calgary to Hawaii. Often, the best parts of the business discussions occur during personal get-togethers. Franchisees from across the country talk together over dinner or beside a pool, get to know one another, and find that their own problems are not as unique as they had thought. Other franchisees who had been down that troubled road could provide helpful answers.

The Tim Hortons ideal of a family working together to help one another embraces the administrative side of TDL as well. The success of the Tim Hortons chain is also attributable to Ron and Tim's attitude of "us" and "we," not "me" and "I." Ron and Tim believed in the strength of a chain, and Ron carried on this same attitude with his head office staff as well as with the franchisees. Employees might start out as single entities, but when they need help, people in other departments share their seniority and experience to keep junior staff on the right track.

As the store numbers grew, so did the need for a strong head office and warehouse operation. One of the early people that made the business stick together was Ron Fitchett, known warmly as the Bean Counter because he started as the company's external auditor. Ron became an employee in 1972. At first glance, he looked like a stereotypical number-cruncher, with dark-rimmed glasses and a slight "desk hunch." This was offset by his six-foot height plus a build that obviously came from more than just pushing paper clips. Ron started as Controller with TDL, became Chief Accountant, and later served as General Manager of Finance. I worked with Ron during my own early years, and I know that he also wore many other hats, as we all did. Tim Hortons was built on the principles of having a dollar before you could spend it, of having a quality product and giving the public excellent service, and of including in the organization people who were more concerned with the success of Tim Hortons than with thinking first of themselves. Ron Fitchett fits into this category. Like others in management, he believed that one of the company's paths to success was real estate. As the company grew, it purchased more land for the various stores. By remortgaging the original land acquisitions, the company increased its cash leverage, a key factor in gaining the cash necessary for expansion.

Central mass buying and distribution gives the best possible prices on supplies to the franchisees. Owners gain from the strength of a large central buying force to supply them all with tried, tested, and true products to be marketed under the corporate logo. The company, in turn, gains from having quality control over all mixes and supplies. The fresh ingredients, such as eggs and dairy products, are purchased locally by the franchisees. To achieve this union of uniformity and economy, the TDL group developed its own warehousing facilities. The first warehouse, part of the new complex on Sinclair Road, Oakville, opened in the fall of 1971. As luck would have it, the right person to run the warehouse was available. Alec (Helmut) Strom, had just left his position as a distribution manager with a company that sold yeast products to Tim Hortons. He called Ron Joyce and asked if he knew of any positions open for a man with his skills. Ron replied, "Can you start tomorrow morning?" Alec became Tim Hortons first warehouse manager.

Years later, Ron described how he and Tim learned from their mistakes when they built this warehouse. They designed it with a built-in sloped ramp so a truck could pull in, the door could be closed, and the truck could be loaded or unloaded inside the warehouse. The ramp proved to be a waste of space. Ron and Tim soon learned that just backing a truck up to a loading dock made much

Tim Horton in the original Oakville warehouse, about 1972. TDL

more sense in every way. Once, Ron and Tim bought a light truck with an automatic transmission. Despite Tim's fondness for cars, neither realized that an automatic transmission couldn't perform adequately on any truck called upon to do heavy-duty hauling. Needless to say, they had to replace the truck with something that could handle a Hortons payload.

Alec's position as warehouse manager lasted for nearly three years; then he purchased his first Tim Hortons location, store #34, in Fort Erie. In this new location, the Tim Hortons cake program started in 1973. Store #34 was the first in the system designed with special shelves to display pies, Wilma Strom says. She thought, "Everyone has a birthday. Why don't we make birthday cakes?" Tim Hortons sent her a white cake mix, and Wilma and Alec started making a Boston cream cake in various shapes and sizes. Like other Tim Hortons programs, this one started over the counter slowly and grew with customer demand.

Alec and Wilma had six stores in total when they decided to purchase the stores in Buffalo on October 16, 1989. On October 16, 1995, they sold the Buffalo stores back to TDL and bought two more Canadian stores, giving them eight stores in all. On April 26, 2003, store #34 marked its thirtieth year of operation. The Stroms' grown children threw a great anniversary party for their parents. I was fortunate enough to be invited and shared in the good times and great memories with about sixty other good friends and relatives.

Alec's strongest recollection of Tim Horton was Tim's talking to him about his concern with staying in shape when he retired from hockey. He wanted to install an exercise room in the office building. Eventually, Tim's dream came true in the mid 1990s, when a full exercise facility, including squash courts and a hot tub, was built in the Oakville complex for all the staff.

To serve the increasing number of stores, the Oakville warehouse was enlarged three times between its small beginnings and the mid-1980s. The Moncton warehouse opened in 1979, Calgary's in 1987, the one in Debert, Nova Scotia, in 1990, Kingston's in 1994, and Langley's in 1995. In 1996, the original Oakville warehouse became additional office space, and a new 55,000-square-foot warehouse was built across the road, surrounded by plenty of land on which it could be expanded as needed. In 2001, the Moncton warehouse was closed when its small size made it uneconomical, and since then all Atlantic Provinces shipments have been handled out of Debert. To handle the growing chain of over 2,000 Tim Hortons stores, TDL now operates five warehouses and regional offices in Canada, two warehouses in the U.S., seven massive distribution and office centres, and separate offices in Quebec.

Gary O'Neill (right) and me at my surprise retirement party in Burlington, Ontario, December 12, 2001. BOB CHAMBERS

CHAPTER FIVE

My Partners, the Store Owners

RIGHT FROM MY FIRST DAY at Tim Hortons, from Gary O'Neill's first phone call, I learned two key pieces of information about my new job: I would be working with many owners in the framework of a franchising organization, rather than in the frame-work of managed, company-owned stores; and I would have to manage a thin advertising budget for stores spread over Ontario and the Maritimes.

The first thing I did was to mail out a questionnaire to the store owners, introducing myself and asking for their input: what did they expect to see advertised? what advertising medium did they prefer?

As I expected, the products that owners most wanted to advertise were donuts and coffee, and their favourite medium was television. This reinforced what I believed, but by asking the store owners' opinions, I gained their support and agreement; I was not interested in unilaterally imposing a head-office strategy. The advertising content would be built around the freshness of the product and the convenience of store locations. Alas, however, our very a limited budget restricted us to local print or radio advertising. Store owners liked radio, too, and we could use that medium to support our other advertising.

We could also afford to upgrade the point-of-purchase material in the stores to reflect the ever-changing product lines. I learned to make the POP dollars go further by photographing and printing the various food products in full colour but setting the words in black ink only. Thus there would be only a one-colour plate change to print for our single store in Quebec, which had opened only four months before my arrival. As well as being an economical way to produce English materials, the method gave us a way to supply French materials at a reasonable cost.

In December 1977, seventy-five store owners attended the TDL annual meeting. There were now sixty-eight stores in Ontario, one in Rosemere, Quebec, twelve in the Maritimes, and two in Newfoundland for a total of eighty-three stores in the system. (Our first western location would open four months later in Penticton, British Columbia, in April, 1978, and the second opened in Surrey, British Columbia, in May. Thus Tim Hortons became a national company, with stores thinly stretched from Surrey to St. John's, Newfoundland.)

This December meeting was my first chance to meet a group of people that I would get to know well over the years. Unlike Black's, which was run by salaried employees, Tim Hortons was over ninety-five per cent franchises, stores owned by people who had put down thousands of dollars to own their own business. I admit now that I was a nervous wreck before that first meeting. Ron Joyce had warned me that the store owners might be hostile toward advertising promotions, and my first succinct call from Gary O'Neill made me realize that his warning would likely come true. It was a great way to begin a new career.

Armed with flip charts and storyboard concepts for print advertisements, I walked to the front of the room after Ron had introduced me. "I think we've got the right person this time," he said. I had hoped for somewhat stronger support from my new employer; obviously I would have to prove myself all around. I proceeded to present plans and suggestions for making the most of the owners' advertising dollars in the 1978-1979 season ahead.

There were no arguments. There was no hostility. In fact, there was general acceptance of my ideas. I believe my initial questionnaire showed the owners that I would listen to their requests, and the fact that the position of Advertising Manager was now filled after a six-month gap gave me a reasonably sound start and enabled me to avoid any residual hard feelings.

Before this meeting, Ron had met with about ten store owners in the immediate Ontario region at the Oakville head office. One of the items on the agenda that evening was a plastic coffee mug Ron had seen in an American coffee shop. This, he felt, could be a great way to get our company free advertising and improve coffee sales. We needed something like this, and the store owners were there to give their input, right from the beginning. The Tim Mug was born, and the project would turn out to be my first big assignment with the company.

There were good reasons for spending time and money on developing a plastic travel mug. The cup was reusable and would feature our name. We could, and did, tie in the initial sale of the Tim Mug to a special offer: a donut and the Tim Mug filled with coffee, all for $1.25. In the late 1970s, few cars and trucks had built-in cup holders, this mug would have a small base that the customer could easily attach to the dash. This novelty item would attract attention, becoming an ad for Tim Hortons in every Tim Mug owner's car. We would be the first donut and coffee chain in Canada to offer such a mug-and-coffee deal. This groundbreaking

FREE COFFEE AND DONUT!

A delicious mug full of Tim Horton coffee and a donut are included at the time you buy a Tim Mug for $1.25. It's a giant-sized reusable cup with snap-on lid that keeps your coffee warmer, l-o-n-g-e-r ! !

TAKE HOME A TIM MUG — ONLY $1.25. GREAT FOR CAR, HOME AND CAMPING.

A 1978 advertisement for the original Tim Mug, sold with a coffee and donut. RB concept got our name and product in front of a lot of Canadians who might never have noticed a Tim Hortons location before. The little Tim Mug became a miniature three-dimensional billboard as it travelled merrily along on the dashboards of thousands of cars in Canada.

Just to get the name right was a challenge. In 1976, Timbits had been introduced. (Contrary to popular opinion, Timbits are not leftover donut centres. In their variety of flavours, Timbits are a separate mix, made independently of donut production.) "Timbits" — all one word — had been named, not by an advertising agency or marketing group, but by Layton Coulter, who was the Construction Co-ordinator at the time. It seemed like a natural evolution to call our coffee mug by a similar name, but would that be all one word, "Timug," or two words, "Tim Mug"? The first version sounded more like a grunt than a proper name, so we chose the two-word version.

When we introduced our muffin program in 1981, we went through the same thought process. Just as with the Timbits and the Tim Mug programs, our very economical research consisted of management and store owners getting together and selecting a new brand name. This time, unlike with "Tim Mugs," "Timuffins" looked and sounded just fine with one "m" missing, and thus we developed another new brand name. And since it included the word "Tim," it, like our other product names, tied directly back to the company.

Part of my new job was to present ideas such as these to the store owners. We had two separate areas in which meetings were held, Ontario and the Maritimes. In Ontario, it was not difficult to get the store owners to come to Oakville or drive to meet them on their own turf, but organizing meetings with store owners in the Maritimes was more difficult. Costs were a concern. We did have a company plane, a twin-engine Beechcraft Duke, and a company owner who could fly it, plus the services of a professional pilot as well. It was more economical for a few of us from the Oakville office to go to many franchisees than to have many franchisees fly to Oakville. Meetings would be scheduled for Halifax, and the head office contingent would fly there on the appointed day.

The plane was stored at the Hamilton airport because of lower hangar and runway fees, the potential for quicker take-offs and landings, and Hamilton's better proximity to most of the staff than Toronto's Pearson or Island airports. The day before we were to leave, Ron would line up the participants he was thinking of taking against an office wall and ask us and himself how badly each of us was needed at the meeting. The twin-engine aircraft would hold four comfortably plus a pilot and a co-pilot. We did not have a co-pilot, so I often got the chance to ride "shotgun." There was also a jump seat right against the door and a small seat that concealed a toilet. Once we had demonstrated our importance to attend the East Coast meeting, we organized our materials, set up car pools to cut the costs of driving to the Hamilton airport, and arranged a rendezvous for the next morning. I usually drove straight out to the hanger because I lived nearby.

On the day of such a meeting, I would be up around five-thirty, leave before six, and arrive at the airport no later than six-forty-five for "wheels up" at seven. Neither fog nor poor weather impeded us. I remember taking off more than once when we could hardly see the nose of our aircraft because of the Hamilton Mountain fog.

Once airborne, we might share a box or two of donuts if someone had had time to pick them up. Ron would often remark on how rare it was to find a plain cake donut (called "old fashioned plain" in the stores) among a dozen assorted donuts. Mostly the store staff would pack yeast-raised donuts, with their various coatings and flavours. Ron is pictured on the cover of the *Toronto Golf 2003* magazine included with the April 25, 2003, issue of the *National Post* as "one of Canada's wealthiest men [who] turns his attention to the links." He is holding a golf club across his right shoulder. On the shaft of the driver are neatly threaded two plain cake donuts. I guess his taste in donuts hasn't changed.

We drank coffee or other beverages at our own risk, since we had at least a three-and-a-half-hour flight with no washroom landings and only the crudest of toilet arrangements. When we were about an hour from Halifax, we would use an air-to-ground telephone that worked intermittently to call the store owners, who would meet us at the airport with their cars.

Meetings started around noon. Because Halifax, in the Atlantic time zone, was an hour ahead of us, we would arrive with little time to spare and proceed immediately to the meeting room at the hotel. The pilot usually stayed with the plane. The meeting would start as soon as we had our equipment ready. This usually consisted of a slide projector, a flip chart, and possibly some show-and-tell items. We usually created "leave-behinds," samples related to upcoming marketing plans that we could give the store owners.

Following the East Coast meetings, we would tour the Halifax area, visiting stores and checking new site locations. Then it was back to the plane, returning to the airport no earlier than midnight, Atlantic time. With the hour we gained flying west, we would land in Hamilton around three a.m., and I'd be home around four. The office opened at eight-thirty, and everyone was expected to be present and on time, regardless.

Because we were trying to control costs, we seldom stayed

overnight, rarely ate three square meals, and almost never took cabs. We followed this pattern of travelling for years, discovering to our dismay that flying around in a corporate aircraft was nowhere near as glamorous as it might seem.

I have always enjoyed the company of Maritimers. In the mid 1980s, when we opened another new section of the Oakville warehouse, the folks from the East came to the festivities. Following the ribbon cutting outside the new loading docks on that summer afternoon, out came the live lobsters and boiling pots, and they made us all a feast of lobster and corn on the cob. Ron Joyce made sure that traditional Maritime hospitality had a place in Ontario. At my retirement party, on December 12, 2001, the Falconer family, who own more than eight stores along the Nova Scotia shore of the Bay of Fundy, presented me with a poem written by Fred Falconer. Here is one of the stanzas:

Your trips down east, three or four times a year,
When the work was done, there was lobster and beer.
It was party time, and we took you in,
We treated you just like one of our kin.
We knew, of course you were from away . . .

No matter how hard Maritimers worked, no matter how successful their businesses were, they never lost sight of the fact that we were all in this together, and life is "some good" if you don't take yourself too seriously. It took a while for this Toronto city slicker to appreciate the friendships that were offered to me.

Sometimes using the company plane was downright harrowing. In early December, 1978, we flew to Thunder Bay, where I was going with Jim Flemming to help with the celebrations involved in opening the hundredth store in the chain. It was so cold that the rivets on the *inside* of the aircraft were covered with ice. Since, for a change, the two of us were the only passengers, I took advantage of the extra space and stretched out across the rear bench seat, covered with my heavy winter coat. A short while later, I woke up in a semi-lit cabin. The interior temperature had dropped. I looked toward the forward portion of the aircraft and saw our pilot, Barry McSween, tapping the gauges on the dashboard.

"What's happened to the lights and heat in here?" I asked Barry.

"We've got a slight problem with one of the engine's generators. Thought at first it might be one of these gauges. Apparently not."

"So where are we?"

"Over Lake Huron."

"How far over Lake Huron?"

"Seven thousand feet up and about in the middle of it."

"And what might you want to do about this problem?" I asked.

"Well, we have twin engines. It appears that the generator on one engine is not functioning properly. It was supplying power for the interior lighting and the heat in the cabin. The other generator is supplying the power for the navigational and radio transmitter systems. We can switch the good generator to heating and lighting inside, or leave it as it is so we know where we're going and how to get there."

"Sounds like a plan," I said.

"I might add," said Barry, "that we should land in Sault Ste. Marie and see about getting repairs."

"Now, that's the best idea of all."

Calls were made and buttons pushed, and we touched down late at night on a very cold runway, with icy winter winds to add to the night's fury. We taxied directly into an open hangar. The engines went down, the hatch was opened, and we stepped out into the safety and relative warmth of that Sault Ste. Marie hangar.

My faith in aircraft, in Barry McSween, and in aircraft personnel in general was very high, but I must confess that my confidence was somewhat shaken when the tall, lanky mechanic reached inside our plane and pulled out what appeared to be a very large Beechcraft Duke service manual to learn how to get the engine cowlings off. As we stood there wondering whether to stay in the Sault that night or take a commercial flight to Thunder Bay, the answer was given to us. I looked through the window in the hangar door and saw the tail of an Air Canada jet slide slowly past in the runway lights, a shark's fin in a swirling sea of snow. It was the last commercial flight out that night. Because of the storm, the major hotels were full. A local cabby took us to a small and, to put it as politely as possible, somewhat quaint motel, where we spent the night.

The opening of Tim Hortons one-hundredth location on December 12, 1978, was a landmark not only within the company but in Thunder Bay as well: Eleanor Miller, the mayor of Thunder Bay, turned out for the celebration. One of my unofficial duties was to take pictures, using my old skills from Black's to record special Tim Hortons occasions. But on that December day, I fell heir to another memorable task. A long cloth banner was to hang outside the store at one end of the building announcing "Tim Hortons 100th location!" I was assigned the risky job of climbing to the roof to install it. Being a city boy, I had dressed for the occasion in leather street shoes and a winter topcoat over my suit, not the best outfit for clambering around in a howling wind on a snow-covered roof. Once up there, I found, buried under two feet of snow, some concrete blocks left over from the construction of the building. These would, they told me, hold down the ropes at each end of the sign. I could have used some ropes myself. Eventually, I got the sign installed, but you may be sure that I left removing it to someone else. I hope whoever did it waited for a warm spring day.

I also learned that day to keep out of Jim Flemming's way when he was baking. An expert at doing the baking for store openings, he never tolerated others getting underfoot. I didn't stay out of his kitchen too well that day, and I nearly ended up hanging on one of the donut racks. In looking back, I guess I could have smoothed the waters somewhat by asking fewer questions of Jim at the time and not expecting him to change position so I could "get a better shot."

We didn't spend all our time together in the snow. In March, 1979, I organized an off-shore company convention in San Juan, Puerto Rico. At one of the business meetings, I made a fateful error with the store owners. I was still working hard to prove myself, so I tried to make sure that business would come first and fun second, in spite of the fact that we were meeting at a wonderful resort in the tropics. I stood up and informed all present to be sure to be on time the next morning, in this very meeting room, for a nine o'clock marketing presentation. About two the next morning, the phone rang in my hotel room. "Is this Mr. Ron Buist?" my caller asked.

"Yes," I mumbled, roused from a deep sleep.

"Mr. Ron Buist of Tim Hortons?"

"Yes," I repeated.

"Mr. Ron Buist of Tim Hortons who is having a nine o'clock meeting this morning?" the sweet female voice asked.

"Yes, I am," I repeated, sensing trouble.

"Well, you can take your meeting and stick it where the sun don't shine!" she said, amongst gales of laughter from her and the

The Tim Hortons convention for store owners, management and suppliers, held in San Juan, Puerto Rico, in March, 1979. Ron Joyce is standing on the extreme right, I'm standing on the extreme left, my wife, Mary Ann, is third from the left in the front row, and the faces of Florence and Ed Mattatall are visible above the middle of the banner. RB

others gathered with her in one of the hotel rooms. The phone went dead, and, in my mind's eye, so did I.

Nine o'clock came, and everyone showed up for the meeting, but suppressed laughter rippled through my audience. I was sure the word had spread about the notorious phone call. The day wore on, and eventually the caller identified herself, an East Coast lady who taught me very succinctly that day how to get the job done without taking life too seriously. The problem was not that the store owners weren't interested in marketing and advertising programs, it was that I had the order wrong: fun first, then business, and then more fun afterwards. It was a worthwhile lesson from someone I now call a friend.

Other vacation-conventions followed, including Las Vegas in

1980 and Florida in 1983 and 1985. Fun was a definite part of the franchisees' menus when they could get away from their stores. They enjoyed the company of their peers, especially during a party at which they could enjoy the fruits of their labours. They allowed me to learn more about themselves and about the Tim Hortons psyche, and thus how best to develop marketing programs. To listen to the franchisees was to listen to our customers right across Canada.

The Oahu, Hawaii, convention in 1987 stands out in my mind more than any of the others. I served on a committee with Peter Moffat, who was camp director for the Tim Horton Children's camps, Ron Joyce, and Michele (Thornley) Allison to arrange the convention. One of Peter's responsibilities was to create a gala party to help celebrate the convention's theme, "Success Through Fresh Ideas." Built around *M.A.S.H.*, the popular TV series, it turned out to be the most memorable company party I ever had the pleasure of attending.

Peter had worked from his Oakville office with the Hawaiian tourist board to arrange for a party site big enough to accommodate 150 store owners, suppliers, and TDL staff. He had obtained the various necessary permits and permissions for the party to take place on one of the island's many beaches. With two weeks to go, the Hawaiian tourist board contacted Peter to tell him that the location was no longer available. The board had become concerned about the ecology and the potential damage such a concentrated group could do to the beach and surrounding areas. Peter had all the pieces in place, from food and bands to a serving staff and special lighting, but now he had no place to put them. Finally, with the help of the tourist board, he discovered a more suitable site, a special inland park. Again, permits were issued, and this park, surrounded by tall trees and tropical vegetation, was ready for our crowd.

The mood of the party had obviously spread to the store owners, especially one in particular. Early in the afternoon before the party, I saw Alec Strom in a ladies' boutique in the hotel. I assumed that the red dress he was looking at was for his wife, Wilma. They are a

Wilma and Alec "Klinger" Strom at the *M.A.S.H.* party held during the "Aloha" convention in Hawaii, January 28, 1987. COURTESY OF ALEC STROM very close couple, and it seemed quite normal for Alec to be there picking out a dress for Wilma. Later that afternoon, I was in the hotel lobby helping our guests onto the buses that would take them to the party. Standing near one of the hotel elevators, I saw a sight that would be burned in my mind forever. The elevator doors slowly parted, and there, standing proudly alone, was Alec Strom. He looked splendid, dressed in that little red dress I saw him looking at, complete with white pumps, nylon hose over what appeared to be shaved legs, a white summer purse draped over his left arm; he had topped the whole ensemble with a floppy white hat. He was a perfect Klinger.

He stood there, a warm smile fixed on his face. I roared with laughter as Alec gathered his courage to emerge into the lobby. Caution overcame him, and he did not move from the spot. The elevator doors slowly closed, and the vision of Alec Strom temporarily disappeared to an upper floor of the hotel. Eventually, he made his dramatic entrance at the party, and afterwards he said that he must have posed as Klinger seventy-five times with the other guests. Years later, he told me that he had not only picked out the dress in the ladies' shop, he had also tried it on. The manager came over to Wilma and asked, "Is this man for real?" She replied, "Oh, yes!" Every family has one; so does Tim Hortons. They're called good sports, and both Wilma and Alec fit into that category.

The Tim Hortons conventioneers left the Waikiki Hyatt Regency Hotel aboard their buses and drove up through the sun-streaked pineapple and sugar cane fields to our remote park site, the winding roads becoming narrower and narrower until we reached the entrance. Although it was still afternoon, the heavy foliage surrounding the entrance made it quite dark. As the bus doors opened, party staff dressed in dark green army fatigues rushed up to put dog tags around our necks:

M.A.S.H. Party
Tim Horton
Convention
January 28, 1987

We walked along a narrow path to a clearing in which we found Army tents and chow tables, and camp benches faced a stage ready for the evening's USO show. Suddenly the air reverberated with the sound of a low flying helicopter. The machine drifted down toward the treetops and madly disturbed every loose leaf and blade of grass as it made a lazy circle over the clearing and attempted a landing. The pilot changed his mind, and the whirlybird headed away from the party site. Fifteen minutes later, a 1950s army ambulance came roaring through the bush and stopped in the middle of the clearing. Two orderlies jumped out, opened the back doors, and, to loud laughter, produced Ron Joyce on a stretcher.

We found out that the pilot had said to Ron, "Do you want to die?"

"Not right now," he replied.

"If I put down in this grove of trees, I doubt if we'll make it. If you really don't want to die, we'll head back to the beach." There they were met by the old ambulance, and Ron made his entrance by land instead of by air, carried off the ambulance on a stretcher, laughing at his own arrival.

Several minutes later, as everyone enjoyed the party, another helicopter approached and hovered over the centre of our group. The side door slid open, and under the swirl of the rotors, thousands of orchids were pushed from the chopper, raining colourfully down on the conventioneers.

Dinner was served into tin army trays. The food was great, even if the dinnerware was questionable. After a sumptuous meal, the stage came alive with the characters from *M.A.S.H.* — Radar, Hot Lips, and Klinger look-alikes mingled at Rosie's bar, and a trio looked and sounded just like the Andrews Sisters. Near the end of the show, the power went out. I don't know whether it was intentional or accidental, but I do know that the man who played Radar put on what appeared to be the best ad-lib rap presentation I have ever seen for the next five or ten minutes, until the power was restored.

Finally, the evening was drawing to a close. The singers and performers returned to the little stage for one last hurrah. From the back of the large tent, Ron Joyce appeared.

"How much to keep going?" he asked.

"Well, it's getting late, and we've done everything," a band member replied.

"You're not listening. How much to keep going?" Ron repeated.

"Well . . ."

Ron produced a large roll of bills and began to peel them off. Much to the delight of all present, the troupe played on and on and on. On that unforgettable night, I learned that Tim Hortons store owners and suppliers not only knew how to work hard, they knew how to play hard, too.

A strip of uncut cups of the current design, showing the format and the margins that inspired the Roll Up the Rim to Win contest idea. RB

CHAPTER SIX

Roll Up the Rim to Win
Eight Years to an Instant Idea

MARKETING PROGRAMS, LIKE CONVENTIONS, had to be well planned and rewarding to the store owners. The Roll Up the Rim to Win contest, now probably the most popular contest in Canada, had been introduced just one year before the Hawaiian convention. Tim Hortons has given away millions of prizes since the contest began in 1986 — cars, vans, and SUVs, televisions, stereos, and cameras, barbecues, and bicycles, and over a hundred million donuts, cookies, muffins, and cups of coffee. Where did the idea come from? Here's the "Tale From Under the Rim" about Roll Up the Rim to Win.

In 1985, Ron Joyce and I both believed that our takeout cups were one of our best vehicles for advertising. Everyone who bought a cup of coffee saw the ad on the cup. Everyone with a cup of coffee in his or her hand acted as a walking billboard. Cups could be printed with any message, and the cost for plate changes in the process of printing cups was minimal, part of the manufacturing cost regardless of the message. At that time, most customers bought our regular-sized cup of coffee, and we wanted to encourage them to buy coffee in the larger-sized cup. TDL wanted to reward customers who purchased our large coffees, but, as always, economy was a corporate obsession. It occurred to us that we could use the cups themselves to offer the prizes that would be the incentive to try a familiar product in a different size. When we proposed the idea to the store owners, they agreed to contribute Tim Hortons products to most of the lucky winners and to permit head office to provide the other prizes that would be advertised through their stores.

How could we organize an exciting promotion at the lowest possible cost to the store owners? It should attract new customers and at the same time induce our present customers both to participate eagerly and to change their habits and buy a larger cup of coffee. Bill Huntley, a good friend and retired vice-president of finance for Black Photo Limited, once said, "There really is nothing new under the sun, just new variations of old ideas." The truth of this became obvious as we tried to dream up the promotion we needed.

There really are only two types of contests: draws and instant wins. Lotteries are not contests, they are simply a form of gambling in which the players spend money without expecting or receiving any product, only a chance of winning. In Canada, lotteries are strictly regulated; to prove legally that a contest isn't a lottery, the federal government has decreed that winners must answer a skill-testing question correctly before they receive the prize. It's this skill-testing question that separates a contest from a lottery. In the United States, no question-answering is required, on the grounds that the action of entering a contest or the knowledge of how to roll up a rim to seek a prize demonstrates enough skill to show that the game or promotion is a contest and not a lottery.

Think of developing a contest as a three-legged stool. Like a real stool, all the legs of a contest must be of equal length to make it function properly. One leg represents the company, in our case, Tim Donut Ltd. The company has the responsibility of running the contest fairly, and it wants to make sure that the contest produces an increase in sales.

The second leg is the store owners and their customers — who, in this context, are in the same category, since the owners tell TDL what the customers want. With respect to a contest, the customers want the chance to win lots of great prizes. Store owners want a contest that will increase their store traffic, reward their current customers, and do it all at little or no cost.

The third leg is the supplier. Initially, the cup supplier was the only outside participant, but the contest grew because all the prize suppliers knew their products would be fairly represented. The fair and level thinking behind the three-legged stool principle is the premise on which the Roll Up the Rim to Win contest was created and became a success.

So what did we have to work with? A company that wanted to increase its sales; store owners who wanted to reward their customers, and customers who wanted an interesting, easy-to-win contest; and a supplier who would understand the intrinsic value of the contest. In 1985, TDL did not yet regularly use an advertising agency that could develop a contest. Instead we had our own in-house brains, such as they were, and we had Lily Cup, our only paper cup supplier. I arranged for a meeting with the Lily Cup sales representative, Roger Wilson, at our Oakville office on the afternoon of September 4, 1985. It would prove to be a very important get-together. I went into the meeting with only the premises that we wanted a contest involving our take-out hot drink cups, and that this contest should increase sales and customer loyalty. I had next to no knowledge of the paper cup business. This was about to change.

The meeting was held in a boardroom with the affectionate title of "The Dungeon," since it was in the basement, directly under the main reception desk. A circular steel staircase wound down to a well–appointed, though windowless, meeting room. The curving twin beams, formed from construction I-beams at the Algoma Steel plant in Hamilton, served as a constant reminder of TDL's roots. In the centre of the boardroom was a round black wooden table. Originally from Ron Joyce's office, it had great sentimental value: it was the table on which he and Tim Horton had negotiated many of their early business transactions. Surrounding the table were typical boardroom chairs, the obligatory phone in the corner, and the white grease-pencil board on one of the textured walls.

Everyone at the meeting agreed that the prize cup was the ideal advertising vehicle. Roger Wilson had brought the necessary show-and-tell item, a roll of uncut paper cups. The roll measured about ten inches across, and it curled around a heavy cardboard tube. We unfurled the roll on the black tabletop so I could understand the process of making paper cups for hot drinks.

The inside of the roll was poly-coated so that, when the cups were cut and formed, they would seal and not leak. The other side, the printable area, featured a parade of our ten-ounce medium-sized hot drink paper cups, printed diagonally to make the best use of the paper roll. They looked something like a series of dress patterns on fabric, before they are cut out and shaped into a three-dimensional form. In three places, I saw white spaces, with a thin black outline: at the top, on the right-hand side, and below each coloured cup pattern. I asked what these areas were for. Roger told me that the white area on the right-hand side was a seam line. The pattern would be cut out to this line, and when the cup was formed, the coloured edge on the left-hand side would overlap the white margin on the right-hand side. This way, the design would butt together neatly, with the white space being used to seal the cup. Well, I asked, what about the outlined white margins at the top and the bottom? The bottom space, Roger said, was called the ledger line, where he would print the name of the manufacturer and technical information about the cup. When the cup was formed, this margin would fold under the bottom edge, forming a little ledger that the cup sits on. The top white margin, he told me, would be curled over to form the lip of the cup.

I asked if you could print anywhere on this side of the roll of paper. Roger answered, "Yes." I then queried whether, if you could print below the ledger line, you could also print under the rim line? Again the answer was yes, with the caveat that anything printed there couldn't be seen when the rim was rolled down to form the cup's lip. At that point, I said, "Thank you very much." I took my new-found knowledge and simply turned one of the phrases around.

If you could not see the printing when the rim was rolled down, you could see it when the rim was rolled up.

The rim was the answer. We didn't need a pull tab, or a separate piece of paper, or something that had to be scratched to enter the contest, any of which would double the paper cup costs to the store pwners. The rim itself would conceal the prizes and make the contest work. I remember that I had one concern as to whether the printing would become illegible when the rim was unrolled. It never proved to be a problem.

That night I worked late trying to come up with a name and theme that would capture this idea. One of the first was "Turn Up and Win," but it sounded too much like a vegetable. "Roll and Win" made little sense, since it wasn't clear what should be rolled. "Roll Up the Rim *and* Win" was getting closer, but it wasn't honest:

"*and* win" suggests that a prize would await everyone who rolled up the rim. I changed the "and" to "to," and that was it: Roll up the Rim to Win — clear, simple, instructive, and entirely honest.

Although I created and named the contest, to this day, the name "Roll Up the Rim to Win" seems long and awkward to me, but the title had to do more than announce a contest. It had to describe the action of the contest itself and advise the customer how to play the game, since, as far as I know, no contest had ever used this concept before. In years to come, the very awkwardness of the title created some of the fun of the game. Today, this long name has entered the national vocabulary.

The first Roll Up the Rim to Win contest (affectionately known within the walls of Tim Hortons as RUTR), was launched in February, 1986. Here is a place where the "KISS" principle, "Keep It Simple, Stupid," really worked. We started very small that first year, doing all the planning on our own. (Actually, we had no choice. In contrast with today's thousands of locations, we were at the time a company of only 246 stores, mostly in Ontario and the Atlantic Provinces, with a thin representation in Quebec and the West.

We had no outside advertising agency or public relations division; our agency was strictly internal. The THD Advertising Agency, totally "in house," was fully accredited by the Canadian Association of Broadcasters (CAB). We placed our own media across Canada, and, as an agency, we received a professional discount. I applied the dollars saved as an internal credit, thereby having an extra funding reserve to put toward our television production.

The first contest would be on the large hot drink takeout cups only, with enough cups supplied to last the stores throughout the month of February. The contest closing date was the end of the year. The prizes were tiny: either a cup of coffee or a snack pack of Timbits. We promoted the first Roll Up the Rim to Win contest only in the stores by means of in-store advertising material.

The prizes were available in a ratio of one in nine: on average, one cup in every nine offered a prize. The customer who tried the larger size of takeout coffee in these contest cups had a good chance of receiving a tangible reward for being a customer of Tim Hortons, and the prize could be claimed immediately at the store. In later years, I heard people say, "I used to win something, but now I don't win anything at all. You've changed the contest." Actually, over the years the ratio of one winning cup in nine has remained quite consistent. I believe that customers originally rolled up the rims somewhat sporadically; now they roll up the rim of every contest cup they get their hands on. They see "Please play again" more often because they play far more often.

Looking back on the very inauspicious start of the Roll Up the Rim to Win contest, I am convinced that the key factors in its success were its simplicity, its low operating cost, and the "first in wins" principle: it was unique and original to Tim Hortons. Because of its longevity, Roll Up the Rim to Win has become a brand unto itself.

Over the years, the faith placed by Tim Hortons management, the store owners, and their customers in Roll Up the Rim to Win has enabled the expansion of the contest. For the first two years, the prizes were all Tim Hortons products. Today, over twenty million customers each year get prizes like a free coffee, donut, muffin, or cookie on the spot. That instant reward keeps the fun in Roll Up the Rim to Win. I wish I had a nickel for every person who has said to me, "I never win anything. All I've ever won is a donut." The truth is, the person has won something — a donut — and the delight of winning keeps people playing.

Even so, in 1988, Paul House, then Vice-President of Marketing (and now President and Chief Operating Officer), suggested that we offer new Jeep vehicles as grand prizes. As the contest rule sheets explained, these major prizes were spread throughout Canada in several general areas, but, because the contest remained random, no one would know the actual stores or where or when they would be won. After the Jeeps, we added televisions and portable phones, stereos, bicycles, and barbecues. The number and variety of prizes grew with the chain: from eleven vehicles in 1988 to thirty in 2003; from 1,500 bicycles in 1993 to 7,500 bicycles in 2003. Lasting products that might be on wish lists — giant-screen TVs, home entertainment systems, and great vehicles and lots of them — have always been the prizes that make the contest exciting for our customers. We never subscribed to the theory that the major prizes should be our own products alone, and this attitude was reinforced by our research on the contest. Basically, our customers determine the prizes they want to receive. We tried to make the prizes something that can be enjoyed by either men or women, prizes that people can use in a wide variety of living accommodations, and finally, prizes that they might put at the top of their list of wants. A wide-screen TV, for example, is something that many would like, but, with all the expenses of our everyday lives, it might not be affordable.

It sounds easy now, but gaining the interest, respect, and involvement of the major suppliers represented in the Roll Up the Rim to Win contests today took years of hard work: pounding on a lot of doors, making innumerable phone calls, drawing up detailed business proposals, and creating persuasive boardroom presentations. Finally, the volume of business that we could guarantee — the millions of cups sold every day, the traffic counts in Tim Hortons stores — secured the involvement of first-rate brands as prize suppliers.

One of the things we could promise these suppliers is non-competitive advertising space within our stores and on our cups. Their products, whether they're cars or bikes, TVs or barbecues, aren't seen side by side with those of their competitors, as they would be in a department store, for instance. They sit by themselves, independent of their competition. Cars offered as prizes are often parked strategically near the stores, with special point-of-purchase advertising promoting both the car and the contest. Tim Hortons has one of the largest customer counts in the quick-service restaurant industry, and many of these customers will consider a particular product in the contest that they might not have even seen before. At least once, a Tim Hortons customer went to the local car dealer supplying the prize car and asked to buy the car displayed at Tim Hortons during the RUTR contest. The dealer sold it right off our lot.

When thinking about any promotion offering any product or service to the public, I like to remember two very important points about customers. First, I consider myself lucky if my advertising and promotion can grab just ten per cent of the customer's attention. No customer is as interested in my products or services as I am. Advertising bombards everyone all day, every day. Studies have shown that in any given twenty-four-hour period, the average Canadian hears and sees over 7,500 brand names and commercial messages, from labels to billboards, on radio and television, in newspapers, magazines, and transit ads, and even on shopping carts and parking garage barriers. To gain entry to the customer's mind takes skill and patience.

Second, customers are all creative to some degree, and a company has to respect that. A contest run for store owners and their customers has to be easy to play and easy to win. The store owners have to be the heroes, personally handing out the prizes to their customers wherever possible. To be palatable to store owners, a contest must be run without increasing costs and making a big dent in their profits.

On January 7, 1986, the introductory correspondence was sent to the stores about the new contest. Headed: "Large Hot Drink Promotion: 'Roll Up the Rim to Win,'" it ran for three pages and had attached to it a sample of the contest entry form. The little form measured just four-and-a-half by six inches, and it was printed on one side only. There was no French version, since the original contest could not run in Quebec due to legal restrictions. Today, with Quebec and the United States included, the large entry form looks like a true and proper legal document. It is — a necessary evil to run the contest properly these days.

In reviewing this original correspondence sent to the stores, I was intrigued by how much of the contest is still the same, over sixteen years later.

Contest Purpose and Advantages

The promotion has been designed to be simply and easily run, directly at store level. The customer has the opportunity to be an "instant" winner, that is, there is nothing for the customer to "mail in" or a time period for the customer to receive their prize.

The (food) prizes are our own products. This allows the store owner/manager to be able to supply from their own product line.

Most of the information in the original letter to the stores holds true today. Head office is completely out of the picture, as far as the customer is concerned. Prizes are still won and are still given by the store owner or operator personally, at the store level. And as soon as Canadian customers answer the legally mandated skill-testing question, they can collect their food prize.

The major prizes, such as vehicles, are pre-ordered and built before the distribution date of the cups that make up the contest. That is why even the colour is stated in the contest brochure and rules. While there is a waiting period for delivery of vehicles and other major prizes, it is minimal. Since the vehicles are all built and ready to go before they are won, all that's necessary is for the car dealer nearest the Tim Hortons store, or the car dealer most convenient to the winner, to be contacted and supplied with the winner's name and pertinent details. The vehicles are then shipped from the manufacturer's storage yard. TVs, stereos, bikes, and other major prizes are purchased by the Tim Hortons advertising fund and stored in the various Hortons warehouses throughout the country. These prizes are then shipped via our own trucks directly to the store that has the winning customer, usually along with the next food order.

The cost of the promotion is still very low for the store owners. While they supply the food prizes, the contest cups, for example, cost the same as their ordinary cups. This was the key factor in the development of the contest, the reason why the idea of simply changing the printing on the cups came to mind, and it remains the same today. At the time of the initial contest start-up, there was no huge advertising budget, and now the normal advertising budget from the store's advertising fund covers the associated costs of the major prizes. The more stores in the system, the more prizes that are offered.

Picture this: I saw a "Roll Up the Rim to Win" winner drive up to the store in his old vehicle, which was literally held together with duct tape and coat hangers. The passenger door was wired shut, the rocker panels were held on with duct tape, and the engine left a blue haze as the car pulled into the parking lot. Promising to collect the old wreck later, the winner drove off in his brand-new van.

One winning family included several children, all very young. The mother was expecting a new addition at any moment, and they had hardly enough room in their old station wagon for the children the family already had. If ever anyone needed a new minivan, they did, and they got one.

A winner once called me to say that she had two Mercedes Benzes and didn't know *what* she was going to do with the van she had won. She took it anyway. In another case, the winner not only didn't have a car but didn't have a valid driver's license, nor could he get car insurance. He, too, took the winning vehicle anyway, but in his case, someone else drove it away.

Winners don't always realize that they've won when they purchase their coffees. One fellow owned a pickup truck and used the space behind the bench seat as a storage area for anything he didn't want. This included a rather large collection of Roll Up cups, and he had never checked under any of the rims. As the contest neared its closing date, he thought he would do a little truck cleaning. He started to remove the multitude of cups and roll up the rims. Under one of them, he discovered that he had won a new vehicle.

Giving away the prizes has not always been an easy task. One winner was an itinerant musician who had won a personal sound system. Try as we might, we could not find her to give her the prize. Although the hunt started in Ontario, it stretched across the country, and she was eventually found, via telephone, in a motel room in Western Canada.

One of my strangest experiences was with a woman who phoned me from a local prison. I initially understood her to say that she was incarcerated and had won a vehicle. I thought that perhaps some visitor had brought her a Tim Hortons coffee in a contest cup. She told me that she could use the phone only at certain restricted times and only for short calls. I remember listening to her hushed tones bouncing off what sounded like concrete walls. My worry about whether this lady could receive her prize vanished when I found out that, yes, she was calling from a local prison, but no, she was not incarcerated. Instead, she was a prison *guard*. We both had a good laugh, and she received her car as easily as anyone else.

In the many Roll Up the Rim to Win contests since 1986, Tim Hortons has given away literally thousands of prizes to the young and the old, the rich and the poor, and almost all of them are thrilled when they realize that the vehicle or TV or bicycle they have just won is really theirs. The prize is not on loan, not on lease, nor is it given only for a limited time. It is really the winner's, no strings attached. There are no strings attached to winning, either. Customers buy only the thing they want, a cup of coffee; they don't have to buy something they may not actually want to get a chance to win a prize, nor do they have to "buy one to get one free." And customers actually win right there in the store, on the spot.

An article in the managing section of the March 24, 1999 *Globe and Mail* recognized that the Tim Hortons Roll Up the Rim to Win campaign "has evolved into an obsession that lures customers year after year" and imagined the mantra "Rrrrroll Up the Rim to Win echoing across the land." Actually, when we first used the "rolling Rs" in a radio commercial, the effect was not greeted warmly by some who had emigrated from Scotland, but Bill Moir, who replaced Paul House as Executive Vice-President of Marketing at Tim Hortons, insisted that we give them another try. When we developed the commercials the following year, Barry (B.J.) Jones, then creative director with Enterprise Creative Selling, our agency at that time, made sure the effect of the "rolling Rs" was not diluted. The announcer began to imitate a Scottish burr throughout the entire commercial, but Barry put an immediate stop to this. He told the announcer, "Just roll the Rs on the name of the contest, don't try to make the whole commercial 'ethnic' by using a burr through the whole read." Everyone accepted the concept, and it finally took off. The *Globe* article cites one of our most memorable television commercials: "Border Guard." In it, a supposed "true Canadian" proves his citizenship by being able to roll his Rs in the Roll Up the Rim to Win phrase. Tim Hortons and the Roll Up the Rim to Win contest had become part of the Canadian culture. Success can have its annoying side to some people, however. The following lighthearted article by Steve Erwin appeared in the *Sun* newspapers on July 14, 1999:

Horton Hears a Boo from Customs

Rrrolling through the border with a cuppa joe and a cute slogan won't win you any special favours at Canada Customs stops.

Border officials have been doing a double-double take at drivers shouting the "Rrroll Up the Rim to Win" catch phrase . . . made popular by a recent Tim Horton Donuts ad campaign depicting a coffee-loving Canadian. It's left a foul flavour in the mouths of some guards who'd rather see a new phrase brewed. "You get sick of it after you hear it half a dozen times," admitted Greg Patterson, a customs superintendent at a Prescott border crossing into the U.S. "But it's just people being friendly." The commercial, part of a contest where caffeine fanatics can roll up the rims of their cups for a shot at an instant prize, features a Canadian driver proving he's a Canuck by rolling the right phrase off his tongue.

But border official say they aren't surprised to hear the one used by the odd java joker among hundreds of cars passing through each day.

"It's inevitable, isn't it?" said Mark Pergunar, a customs superintendent at a Thousand Islands crossing near Lansdowne. "It's becoming a pop culture icon."

All jokes aside, customs officers don't seem too concerned that some smart-mouthed motorist might stir an international incident.

"It's not like there's this great wave of people saying it," Pergunar said. "It has occurred, but not to the point of getting obnoxious," he said.

"Border Guard" was not the only RUTR commercial that was fun to shoot and see on the screen. We had good times with other spots as well. One of these stands out in my mind. We planned to feature an SUV as the major prize. We had ordered this vehicle with a certain type of wheels, we had done the still photography, and now the television commercial had to match, because we were sticklers for "what you see is what you get." Even the colours were predetermined, and we never used the phrase, "similar to model shown." As we prepared to shoot the commercial, we discovered that the wheels did not match our still photography.

This problem should have been easy to fix. We called around Toronto, where the commercial was being shot, and found a dealer who had the right type of wheels on a wrong-coloured SUV. No problem. We talked the dealer into loaning us his vehicle. We hurriedly brought it down to the street outside the studio. We jacked it up, stripped off its wheels, and rolled them into the studio. Next, we prepared to take the wheels off the prize SUV sitting in the studio. Oops. Someone forgot to put in the vehicle the special tire wrench that would fit this particular unit. The wheels would not come off. Meanwhile, the entire crew sat around, waiting and watching and listening to the clock tick as the cost of the shoot climbed. Finally, in desperation, we cut the wheels off with an acetylene torch. We "dummied" up the new wheels, and at last we managed to complete the shoot.

Roll Up the Rim opened the door to many weird contacts with the general public. A contest open to over thirty million people was bound to attract some of the more eccentric ones, and over the years I began to categorize some of my most interesting telephone callers.

The Heavy Breathers

These people would call me and announce, in very quiet tones punctuated by heavy breathing, "I know where the prizes are." They had decoded the "system" in the printing of the cups that identified which ones had prizes under the rim. This intrigued me, since there was no "system" or method of identification that could tell anyone what was under the rim. Some of these callers would threaten to go to the media. Patti Jameson, Vice-President of Tim Hortons Communications, had the best answer to this one: "Please, go ahead and tell the media. We know that no identification is on the face or any other part of the cup. Your telling the media will only help to increase awareness of the contest. Thank you sincerely for your interest in Tim Hortons." Patti was right. No customer ever made a "report" to the media, or at least no media ever followed up on such a report, since there is no truth to it.

Lost Rim Tabs

I wish I had a dime for every phone caller who said, "I have a winning tab, I kept a photocopy of it, the staff saw me with it, I can't find it now, can I still have the prize?" I found that the best answer was this: "If you substitute the words 'winning rim tab' with 'five-dollar bill,' would you expect a bank to give you a new five-dollar bill to replace the one you lost?" Keeping a photocopy is a personal reference. If the company started to honour photocopies of the winning tabs, the number of winners would be endless. Winners should treat a winning tab as cash.

The Lawyer

No, this is not a lawyer joke. It describes the "lawyers" who called me with this story: "I represent so-and-so, who purchased six coffees for a crew of men who are working on his house. One of these workmen received a winning tab for a van / bicycle / barbecue. Since my client purchased the coffee, we believe he is entitled to the prize." The first thing I did was write down the name of the "lawyer" so I would never use his or her services personally. The second thing I did was advise this "lawyer" that the person who turns in the rim is the winner.

The Screamer

One customer truly stood out from the rest because of the very nature of his phone calls. For about three years in a row, I received the same call from the same man, yelling so loudly that I could put the receiver down on my desk and still hear him clearly. The content of the conversation was not nearly as clear, but this is the heart of what he said: "My doctor says that I can't drink coffee, and you are forcing me to drink a medium coffee to be in your contest."

Try as I might, I could not get through to this man that he could purchase any medium-sized hot beverage and receive a contest cup, or he could send a letter to the address given in the contest rules and receive a contest cup without buying anything. The fact that we had always run the contest on the larger size of cups had no meaning to him at all. He screamed and yelled so much that I thought he would become physically ill. It never happened. After listening to him for a few minutes, I could do nothing but politely terminate the conversation and wait until the next year for his expected phone call. Eventually, one year, I patiently waited for an opening in the conversation and spoke to him by name (it was not hard to remember after years of abuse). I told him that nothing about the contest had changed from last year when he called, and nothing was expected to change in the immediate future. The calls stopped.

In May, 1999, *Marketing Magazine*, the Canadian benchmark of advertising and promotion, ran a cover feature calling Roll Up the Rim to Win a "perpetual promo." The author, Liza Finlay, adds, "Promotions come and go, but a rare few like 'Roll Up the Rim to Win' look like they have enough momentum to run forever." I don't know about forever, but I think it's good for a while yet. Finlay points out that the contest is "working its way into the cultural fabric." She quotes John Lulland, associate professor at the Richard Ivy School of Business, University of Western Ontario, who sees the contest building "long-term loyalty by focusing on rewarding existing customers rather than attracting new ones. [Roll Up the Rim to Win] has beaten the odds by creating clear and attainable objectives employing winning strategies." In other words, if it ain't broke, don't fix it. "The beauty of Tim Hortons promotion is its simplicity – it's easy to play, and easy for the company to finance." Finlay's line of thinking falls right into the three-legged stool principle upon which we originally built the contest: make it fair for everybody, and stick with it.

At Tim Hortons, the belief has always been that a product or service must stand on its own within the confines of the business before it is heavily promoted through the media. Staff members consume countless cakes, pies, donuts, breads, and bowls of soup, tasting, testing, and redoing, before TDL even thinks of launching them in the stores. Then, if the product is good, it will be accepted by the public. If it's not, all the advertising in the world will not make it saleable. The same theory is the key to the success of the Roll Up the Rim to Win contest. In 1992, six years after its introduction, we started advertising it on radio and television. In fact, we didn't even use pole signs outside the stores until the early 1990s. We built the popularity of the contest strictly by rewarding our growing customer base and at the same time maintaining the enthusiasm of the store owners, who saw a marked increase in their traffic and sales. The contest, like Tim Hortons products, had to succeed within the company before we tried to popularize it among people who were not already our customers.

Tim Hortons customers believe in "Roll Up the Rim to Win" as a reflection of the chain's integrity. Here's a tip of the hat to its continued success.

BACKBENCH

This comic strip was first published in *The Globe and Mail* on April 1, 2003.

CHAPTER SEVEN

Broadcasting the Brand

"BROADCASTING" LITERALLY MEANS SCATTERING in all directions, and it is useful to keep this in mind when thinking of advertising. At Tim Hortons, we had to learn to use print advertising, radio and television commercials, and billboards in ways that would be cost-effective and bring customers into the store. First, though, we had to develop public recognition of our name by making our products speak for us. I call this "Broadcasting the Brand."

Tim Hortons offered a much smaller menu when I first started working there in 1977 than it does today, but we sold a wide variety of foods other than donuts. I approached Ron Joyce with the idea that we should change the logo to emphasize the words "Tim

Horton" instead of "donuts." He shot me down in flames: "We are not selling a 'Tim Hortons,' we are selling donuts." In retrospect, I know he was right. At that time, the strength of the company was donuts, which in turn built the brand name "Tim Hortons." The product had to succeed to give the brand name credibility. People had begun to associate the name Tim Hortons with the product, not the other way around, and I was trying to put the cart before the horse.

In the early 1990s, we had the pleasant task of finding out what people though of Tim Hortons, and by then we had the luxury of being able to hire top researchers, like Trevor Collier Research and Donna McPhail, of McPhail Marketing Communications, to help us. Not only that, but we were able to have the creative strategy come to fruition through Enterprise Creative Selling, our advertising agency. Thankfully, the days of one-man-band marketing were over. We had the added brainpower to raise the bar.

The only statistics our research company could give us to measure our own achievements came from the Quick Service Restaurant (QSR) business, but the comparison was not entirely valid. The customer may come to Tim Hortons for a cup of coffee and a donut before work, stop in for a mid-morning break or possibly for lunch, have a private meeting at Tim's halfway through the afternoon, gather socially after an evening meeting, or break a road trip in the small hours of the morning. Customers drop in for a snack or a treat, and their experience has no beverage-meal-dessert pattern with a beginning, middle, and end. They do not make dinner reservations at Tim Hortons; in fact, even today they can hardly be said to dine there, even though the soup and sandwich product line makes it a suitable place for an evening meal. The term "lunch hour," we learned, seldom describes eating for an hour. Instead, people want to eat, shop, and do other errands during their midday time to themselves. That's why the lunch program was built around speed. Tim Hortons was and remains a place to take a break. The company built a whole new restaurant category in Canada, the break-time store.

Customer loyalty is vital to the food business, and turning drop-in customers into regulars plays a major part in the success of a break-time restaurant. However, the amazing popularity of Tim Hortons coffee can be hard even for a Tim Hortons executive to fathom. Once I got into a friendly conversation with a cab driver taking me to the downtown core of Halifax from the airport. When asked, I told him what I did for a living, and my answer prompted him to launch into a tale of desperation. He just couldn't get his coffee to taste the same at home as it did when he bought it at Tim Hortons. He started making his coffee from our brand of ground beans, but it didn't taste good enough. He went to the trouble of taking home some of our take-out coffee cups to drink it from, but still he wasn't satisfied. Next, he was considering a Tim Hortons home coffee brewer.

I believed, and still believe, that the strongest means of advertising food to increase the customer base is television. The product is shown in full colour, and viewers can see it being served and eaten or drunk. Coffee can be poured into a cup, a sandwich can be made, and packaged goods can appear on camera with the ready-to-eat product. Print, packaging billboards, and radio are excellent support media, but nothing beats the movement and appetite stimulation of television.

I compare television advertising to the high-end gambling tables in Las Vegas. You've got to have enough money to step up to the tables before you can even get into the game. Producing a commercial with the assistance of the TV station was one way to get around some of the high costs involved with production. I had used this pattern years earlier to enable Black's Camera Stores to advertise on television, and I used it again when we undertook Tim Hortons television advertising in the early 1980s. But in 1970, long before I joined TDL, CHCH TV in Hamilton developed the first commercial for Tim Hortons, a thirty-second spot produced by Donna Lloyd.

At that time, the Tim Hortons advertising fund had two sources. One part of it came from the Hamilton store owners and was to be spent in the greater Hamilton market, and the rest came from the other store owners in the chain. Since the majority of the stores then were in the Hamilton area, they had a big enough budget to try TV advertising.

The CHCH commercial of 1970 had a lot of nostalgia built into it. Tim wanted to produce it around the theme, "You meet the happiest people at Tim Hortons." He provided the on-camera talent, including himself, George Armstrong, and Pat Quinn, who was born in Hamilton and was then playing with the Toronto Maple Leafs. He included another famous Hamilton athlete in the line-up, Angelo Mosca, from the Hamilton Tiger Cats football club. Tim made another creative decision that haunts this original commercial. Along with the four athletes is a fifth man that neither Quinn nor Armstrong can remember. Angelo Mosca believes that Tim wanted to put a little mystery into the commercial. Realizing that people would recognize the sports celebrities, he invited a young man who was a customer in the store at the time to sit in for the final shot. He intended this fifth man to pique viewers' curiosity, and now, after all these years, the intrigue still exists.

Even though the spot would play primarily in the Hamilton market, the Tim Hortons store #17, on Trafalgar Road, Oakville, was used as the location. Brand new and of the latest design, it was the best to show on camera. Costs were kept to a minimum; Tim's friends probably worked for the donuts and coffee they were seen consuming in the closing shot. The store stayed open while the cameras rolled — nothing could interfere with business. The crew simply waited until after the morning rush and filmed the commercial MOS ("mit out sound," industry slang for "without sound," supposedly in imitation of a German director). Since they didn't record sound in the store, they didn't need to worry about ambient noise. They just rolled the tape and added an announcer's voice-over and music back at the studio.

Despite the relatively low cost, however, the company discovered that, because it had used the budget heavily to produce the spots, it had run short of money to get enough exposure on television. Even if Hortons had the greatest commercial in the world, if the film just stayed "in the can" and didn't get enough air play, no one would see it, no one would hear it, no one would care, and no one would buy. All the same, I felt sure that somehow we had to make TV commercials an important component of our advertising.

In our early years of working together, Ron Joyce and I had different ideas about how to make Tim Hortons more successful. Ron was right to work so hard to develop products that sold well over the counter. Tim Hortons was the only fast food business that emphasized freshness, it stayed open around the clock, and its owner was a major hockey star. The challenge came when we wanted to expand our customer base, which we had to do as the competition increased and as others tried to duplicate the Tim Hortons success story.

The original Tim Hortons customer base was 55% male, mostly blue-collar workers, and 45% female. We wanted to attract more women and a greater economic cross-section while keeping these original customers. A clean store, a well lit parking lot, and clean washrooms, plus loads of fresh product in a friendly atmosphere was the perfect combination. Achieving this goal is a constant challenge, but in the end, this operational strategy worked wherever stores were built. Often I was asked, "What is Hortons target market?" I would respond, "Everybody." That answer is not trite; instead, it reflects the fact that the customer demographic depends on where the stores are located. An owner who opens a store near senior citizens' homes will attract a great lunch crowd enjoying a nutritious, economical meal, just like in other areas. Go downtown in a major city and watch the traffic flow: "yuppies" buying coffee and something sweet. In an industrial area, lots of meals are made in the morning to be someone's lunch on the job; lots of Thermoses are filled for later on in the day. Stores near hospitals, if not right in them, have a strong traffic flow of visitors and health professionals enjoying our products at all hours of the night as well as through the day. Today, the customer base has grown considerably from that 55% blue-collar male / 45% female breakdown to include the people we wanted in our stores . . . everybody.

I believed in television advertising because I knew it could take the message out to those who had never heard of a Tim Hortons Donut Shop. Despite budget limitations, a group of storeowners also wanted to see us back on TV again. In the eyes of some, myself included, Ron seemed to consider advertising a necessary evil. I realize now that what he disliked about advertising, television in particular, were the slick, big-city commercials that often seemed designed by agencies to win awards rather than sell product. He disliked spending a lot of money on a commercial that failed to make the product, or the brand, king. He did not dislike adver-0tising; he disliked costly, inefficient advertising. My task was to make television advertising that would be affordable for our small com-pany, look as effective as other commercials on television, and reflect the company values that Ron was expressing.

I thought long and hard about the obstacles to TV advertising and what TV advertising had to achieve. I recognized that the competition on television is not only the immediate competitors — in this case, similar food outlets — but also everyone else trying to attract the customer's attention: General Motors, Kimberly Clark, Proctor and Gamble, Ford, Coca Cola, and all the other multinationals, as well as every other local business.

Ron was right about brand development: it works from the inside out, not from the outside in. The toughest sell occurs in the three feet across the retail counter between the seller and the buyer. No advertising agency in the world, no TV commercial, radio spot, or print ad can make a poor product sell. Conversely, no advertising agency can take even a good product and make it a continuous success if the commercial over-promises. To gain and keep loyal customers, advertising must be totally honest.

Tim Hortons makes sure a product is developed correctly and accepted over the three-foot-wide retail counter before even considering the need for heavy advertising. A standard business phrase often repeated by Paul House, the current President and COO, says it all: "It is far less expensive to keep the customers you have than incur the high costs of trying to get them back." In today's market, others use the same thinking. Loblaws, one of Canada's largest supermarket chains, has made President's Choice products extremely successful simply by selling them at store level, without major outside campaigns for specific products. They develop a product to their satisfaction, wrap it in a beautifully designed package, and put it on the shelf. If it works, it stays; if it doesn't, it goes. Loblaws seem to have secured a very loyal President's Choice clientele and an expanding customer base without the extra cost of media advertising.

A good market research company conducting sophisticated research is essential to a company with significant resources, especially when coupled with a good advertising agency. Both can be expensive, but maximizing the success of a large company is somewhat like aiming a very large cannon. One degree off the target can prove disastrous. A company as large as today's Tim Hortons needs good strategic research to be able to determine what their customers and those who patronize their competitors think of the company and its brands. However, this large-company philosophy has grown out of the small-company experience. Over-the-counter research is the key, I believe, to making a small company successful. A small company can try a new product, and, if the product leaves something to be desired, the company can pull it off a few shelves and correct the problem.

At Tim Hortons, we embarked on a program of strategic research. Who was our target market? Did we appeal to this market? What was the market's attitude toward our products? How well did they know our products? Had our advertising messages been saying the right things? We tried to get answers to such questions before a full roll-out of a new product across the chain.

We found creative research far more difficult. Strategic research helped us to understand who we were, whereas creative research helped us to figure out how to tell people what we wanted them to know. B.J. Jones once asked, "How do you storyboard a smile?" Without taking credit for this oft-repeated remark, he passed its simple message on to me: creative messages, either verbal or in a storyboard format, leave out the magic achieved with film, actors, sound, and music. This is why I believed so strongly in TV advertising: if the commercial smiles at the customer, the resulting warmth induces the customer to smile back.

The focus groups so essential to creative research often helped correct our direction, not so much by telling us how to do the creative aspect of our advertising as by telling us what was missing. This missing link would have to be incorporated into any TV commercials we might make. At an executive level, we digested the results of our creative research as fully as we could. Then, as an in-house corporate executive, I had to trust the instincts of the experienced creative personnel to achieve the successful sales message, whether in print, on radio, on billboards, or on television.

It would be ATV (Atlantic Television) that got us back on the air. As early as 1978, ATV had contacted me about advertising on television. Store owners like Gary O'Neill, in Moncton, New Brunswick, were anxious to see Tim Hortons on TV. So was I. The problem was that five-letter word: money. As the decade closed, I began to work with ATV sales rep Don Mackay, who helped put a plan together. By 1980, we could start to see our way clear to at least think about using TV advertising again. Keeping cost limitations in mind, we saw that creating commercials showing only our food would mean we wouldn't have to pay talent fees. A voice-over would be simpler and less expensive than an on-camera read. In fact, we could get double value out of a commercial by doing voice-overs in both English and French. This plan would allow us to shoot what is known as a table-top commercial. I worked on the idea of a "camera persona" in which the camera would travel through a variety of Tim Hortons products, such as the donut box, various donuts, Timbits, cold drink cups, and fancy products, and end up looking at a steaming hot cup of coffee in a Tim Hortons mug. This scenario sounded as if it could be produced without too much difficulty, and ATV agreed to make this test commercial for us at their studios in Halifax at no cost to us.

Don and I wanted to make this affordable Tim Hortons commercial and show it to the Maritime store owners at an upcoming regional meeting. It would demonstrate the effectiveness of an inexpensive style of creative content and provide them with an estimate of how much making such a commercial would cost, and we could determine whether they would buy into it with their advertising dollars.

I persuaded Ron that we had a good shot at making this commercial a reality and that we should go ahead with ATV's test. ATV, too, thought it would work, and they hoped the test would convince us to buy air time and commercial space from them in the immediate future. Whatever their policy may be today, back then they believed in the strength and promise of Tim Hortons as much as the store owners did. With Ron Joyce's blessing, I did something unheard of for a Tim Hortons executive at that time. Within days of the planned regional meeting, I took a commercial Air Canada flight alone to Halifax to begin putting this commercial together.

When I arrived at ATV's Robie Street studios, I laid out the script and plans before the producer. We realized that to make this commercial work, we needed a counterbalanced camera crane — a large arm, twelve to fifteen feet long, with a counterweight at one end and a camera mount and seat for an operator at the other end. The arm would allow us to use a snorkel lens, which is like an upside-down periscope that can travel at table level without the cumbersome camera behind it. The camera and all the other equipment would hang from the crane, out of the way and above the eye of the lens. With this arrangement, the camera's eye could travel through Tim Hortons products.

The counterbalanced camera crane looks like a giant teeter-totter. The arm superstructure sits on a heavy metal pedestal mounted on studio wheels, which are designed to glide over smooth studio floors. So much as a cigarette butt on the floor causes this apparatus to jiggle as it is moved. Unfortunately, ATV did not have such a piece of equipment, but luckily the nearby CBC studio did, and they agreed to lend it. Imagine, then, this enormous contraption, designed to be pulled by crew members across a studio floor, being hand-pulled down a back street parallel to Robie Street — no shocks, no springs, just little fat wheels to trundle and bounce over the rough pavement as we pulled it along. I still can see it, wobbling down the road and through ATV's huge back doors like a giant praying mantis, trying to find a home again in a darkened TV studio.

When we got the crane into the studio, technicians fitted it with a television camera, no small job because, in those days, a camera was large enough that two men were required to carry and mount it safely. Later, we began shooting all of Tim Hortons commercials on film, not on videotape, because film is layered, and one set of colours and dyes on top of another gives a softness that is superb for showcasing food. Videotape, a very clear, harsh format, is great for sports broadcasts or selling hardware, but not for communicating the richness of food. However, videotape is considerably cheaper to use than film, so this time, we went with videotape. The balance weights were added to the other end of the arm, and the operator climbed aboard. After setting up all this equipment, the shoot was simplicity itself.

Within a day or two, the rest of the group came down from head office in Oakville and joined the crowd of store owners to go over marketing plans and see this commercial. We used two TV monitors — basically, just a couple of television sets — one on either side of the speaker's podium. On these monitors, the store owners would see a thirty-second test spot that, no matter what happened, would not see the light of day again. We ran the commercial twice, and for the first time, an audience applauded what I had done. They loved the commercial, and they wanted to go ahead with television as part of their advertising package.

Around midnight, the Oakville contingent headed to a car that Ron had rented to drive back to the Halifax airport. If you have ever travelled to Halifax and taken this road to the airport, you know how very black and desolate it is. The airport was built far from the city to avoid fog, and I've been told that someone forgot to explain that the trees that originally stood there helped keep the fog in check. The trees were cut so the planes could land, and the fog rolled in. Now travellers must drive for about half an hour along this highway of bleakness. I was the driver; Ron Joyce sat in the back seat. About halfway to the airport, with all as quiet as a night on the moon, a voice cut through the darkness. It was Ron.

"Ron," he said.

"Yes, sir."

"Do you think they can be trusted?"

"Who do you mean, Ron?"

"The TV station people."

"You mean ATV?"

"Yeah. Do you trust them?"

"Yes, I do."

"Okay. The store owners liked the commercial. Let's do it."

And with that simple conversation, Tim Hortons was about to get back on TV.

The new strategy began the next year, in 1981, with the first Tim Hortons TV commercial that I coordinated. It would introduce Timuffins, and it would play nationally, including on ATV; Don Mackay's faith had not been misplaced, nor our faith in him and the network.

Donna Lloyd, the producer of the 1970 commercial, was still with CHCH TV in Hamilton. I had met her in 1980, when she had moved from production to media sales. Warm and honest, she always gave me the impression that she could work on either side of the camera. Once the decision had been made in Halifax that television would again be part of Tim Hortons marketing plan, Donna was instrumental in helping us get back on air. She directed me toward a man who wore many hats in the business, Jack Kuper, the owner of Kuper Productions. We needed all the necessities to make a commercial, but we did not have an agency to handle this, since we still were working within a very limited budget. I soon found out that Jack would work for us like a one-man advertising agency.

We had already prepared a television storyboard on our new Timuffins, and we asked Jack if he would produce this commercial. Jack did not want to do the storyboard as we presented it to him, but, he said, he would be interested if we allowed him to rebuild the creative on the storyboard. About a week later, he came back with a revised and improved commercial. We bought his work and thus embarked on a relationship that lasted through many commercials, shot from 1981 until 1983. These included commercials for Timuffins, Strawberry Timtarts, and Timbits, and also a generic donut commercial. Jack handled all the details, from the storyboard to editing the film on his own Moviola.

I had studied radio and television production at Ryerson and learned the rudiments of commercial production while at Black's, but it was Jack Kuper who gave me over three years of hands-on commercial production experience, patiently teaching me the nuances of the trade. Working with Jack stood me in good stead when, in the late 1980s, the company's growth enabled me to hire and collaborate with other advertising agencies.

April 1981 was the target date to introduce the public to muffins, or "Timuffins" as we originally called them. We decided to use television as the main advertising vehicle, and I followed the pattern that Ron Joyce and Tim Horton had established years before. To save money, I used talent that included my neighbours, my daughter, and friends of the producer/director. We shot without sound, so no one had lines to speak; it's one thing to smile and nod and bite into a muffin on film, but it's quite another for an amateur to learn and deliver lines as well. The music we used was either in the public domain or on a commercial sound track that we owned outright. We shot in empty warehouses and in Tim Hortons stores during the night, when traffic was low.

We did make one expensive choice: we shot on 35mm colour film to communicate the high quality of the food. Nothing, not even gaining softness by putting a nylon stocking over the camera lens, makes food shot on videotape look as succulent as food shot on film. However, once the richness of food has been captured on

On a 1995 commercial shoot in Quebec. To give final approval for a "travel" shot that would give the effect of a customer driving into a store, I'm sitting in a special rigging on the side of a truck. COURTESY OF RON BUIST

film, it transfers beautifully to videotape, and we did this to keep costs reasonable and make post-production easier.

Our strategies worked. Timuffins got off to a flying start, thanks in part to the commercials, but maintaining the product line had its difficulties. Tim Horton commissaries initially produced the muffins. These commissaries were very large kitchens, each with an operating store on the front. They were strategically located in cities such as Hamilton, Ontario, and Moncton, New Brunswick, to serve a number of stores within their area. At first, commissaries served the stores' needs well, but naturally some stores sold more muffins or sold them faster than others. Then, as new stores opened in their areas, the commissaries found it difficult to keep up with the burgeoning need for muffins. Eventually, the store owners had to dig into their pockets and install on-site bakery facilities so they could produce the muffins they wanted, when they wanted them.

Installing these baking facilities could be harder than it looked. More than once, we had to go to the local supplier of electrical power and have the street transformers replaced so they could supply the stores with the extra power to run their new ovens, as well as their fryers, air cleaners, and air conditioning and heating systems. All for the love of a simple muffin.

After Timuffins, the next new product was the Strawberry Timtart. This launch marked the first time we ever tested a new treat on focus groups before our over-the-counter testing. In this way, we could determine just what the customers would like before we tested the treat on even a small segment of the public. One woman told us, from the other side of the one-way glass, that she wanted to find a strawberry under the custard in the centre of the Strawberry Timtart.

We took this woman's remark to heart, and that's how the Strawberry Timtart was originally introduced. We started with all guns blazing: as with Timuffins, we had a great new product and fresh, new television commercials, and we added to these advantages some great in-store point-of-purchase advertising. It was in the Strawberry Timtarts commercial that baking expert John Lynn made his acting debut as, yes, a baker, carrying a tray of Strawberry Timtarts. It became obvious that we were on the right track, combining high-quality products with the advantages of television advertising, when Tim Hortons had to purchase literally every commercial flat of strawberries in Newfoundland just to keep up with the initial demand.

These first two commercials introduced new products; how could they go wrong? For us, the acid test was to see if we could improve the sales of an existing successful product: Timbits. For our first Timbit commercial, we went off to a local warehouse with our family-and-friends talent, dozens and dozens of Timbits, and a large tilted white board, down which those little round nuggets could roll merrily in the opening shot. We had a winner. The average television commercial uses approximately eight thousand feet of film, two or three days of shooting time, and months of pre-production, not to mention the weeks of editing and sound recording that follow. But I found that I soon forgot the difficulty of getting a commercial in the can if I could see it increasing customer awareness. In the first month the Timbit spot was on air, Timbit sales increased thirty-four per cent.

By this time, business had improved to the extent that Tim Hortons could afford more commercials, but we still had to work as inexpensively as possible. Oftentimes, weather was our greatest foe. Many of our customers remember the "twenty-minute fresh" coffee commercial, often called Snow Plow, which told the story of a snow plow driver who cleared the way for himself and others to get to Tim Hortons for a cup of fresh coffee. We shot it in a Hortons location on top of the Hamilton escarpment in the dead of winter. The story took place at night, so we started at sundown. That night brought the only major snowstorm that the Hamilton area had had that winter — blinding, fine snow, swirling around the store. Sandbags were brought in to secure the various pieces of equipment that lit and shielded the building for the outdoor shots. The klieg lights shook in the wind. The snow was so fine that it didn't even show up on camera, so we had to create an artificial snowstorm in the midst of the real snowstorm. A good part of the prep time was spent installing two old air-cooled Volkswagen motors, mounted on stands, to act as giant fans. Two crewmen in front and two behind each engine threw dry potato flakes in front of the roaring blades to create the snowstorm effect.

It was quite a sight. It was, in fact, a very silly Canadian moment: making fake snow while the real stuff blew all around us. The night was exceptionally cold. The crew members were bundled up in winter coats and rain gear to protect them, not only from the artificial wind, but from the real cold and the real wind of this winter's night. Their heads were wrapped in scarves, toques, and anything else that was handy.

The Volkswagen engines roared.

Up went the potato flakes.

The camera rolled.

The "snowflakes" looked great in front of the camera as the snow plow and driver arrived on cue. Unfortunately, they did not look so good on the front of the store or all over the tile inside the store, where the cast and crew tracked them from the shoot outside. We left the store well after sunrise with a great commercial in the can, but we had to leave behind us a special clean-up crew to strip and entirely refinish the store's floor.

On another occasion, we went out west to shoot a commercial to promote our new soup line, using the Canadian cycling team and the rugged beauty of the coastal mountains where they were training. We found out why British Columbia is sometimes called the "wet coast." The technical crew had gone on an advance scouting mission and had selected the camera positions. All would have proceeded smoothly had we been able to *see* the camera positions. It rained. It rained some more. It rained for days on end. In fact, the rain never stopped.

Camera positions that had been set up over little mountain streams disappeared under raging torrents pounding down the mountain. Natural bridges — gone. Camera positions — gone. The mountains — we couldn't see them for the fog and rain; they might as well have been gone. We began to wonder about the purpose of our heavy rain gear. It sealed our bodies from the rain, but it also sealed our bodies from the air. We were as soaked on the inside as we were on the outside. Everything I had was wet. I felt like a vertical fish. But we got a great commercial.

This particular commercial was actually shot halfway between

This scale model toy truck shows the mobile billboard effect of Tim Hortons advertising on highway trailers. The toy is a prototype and was never sold in the stores. RB

Vancouver and Whistler on the Sea and Sky Highway. Joanne Stewart, the account director of our agency, Enterprise Creative Selling, played a major part in this commercial shoot (and many others). Vancouver was her hometown, and she was glad of the chance, however short, to visit her parents. While we were making these television commercials, she and I traveled from Lunenburg to Vancouver and a lot of spots in between. Many of my anecdotes about our shoots are based on Joanne's recollections. Joanne is the one who called the West Coast the "wet coast" and the Sea and Sky Highway (due to be improved for the 2010 Winter Olympics) the "Scream and Die Highway."

I would find out years later that Joanne had one job she found somewhat trying. Along with her coordination duties in threading the agency and client relationships smoothly together, she had to keep an eye on the client, me. It seems I had a bad reputation for wandering around the set. My interest in seeing how everything was done was not for the purpose of checking up on others, but to learn for myself. To the best of my knowledge, I always managed to be back near the camera to approve a shot or help with a product display call. Joanne put up with my wanderings, never complaining. I believe we made a great team, and she is even a help to me now in refreshing my memory about a lot of the things that happened during our many commercial shoots together.

One reason for the success of Tim Hortons TV commercials may be that they reflect the fundamental honesty of Tim Hortons products. We always used real donuts in our shots, so real that, whenever the floor director would announce at the end of the last day, "It's a wrap. Thank you, everybody," there would be a mad dash for the showcase full of donuts. They might have been sitting under the lights, but they still looked mighty good to the working crew. When we could arrange it, we would give away the donuts and pastries to a local Salvation Army or group home, where the treats would be enjoyed by people who might not be able to buy them. In a soup or sandwich commercial, the same rule applied. The sandwiches would be made on set minutes before shooting so they'd be at their peak of freshness. I was told by more than one food stylist on set that, when shooting a soup commercial, some other companies put marbles in the bottom of the bowl to give the soup a fuller appearance. Tim Hortons soups are prepared on set to be exactly the same product that you would purchase in a store.

Television commercials may be the gold standard in advertising, but radio commercials have always helped Tim Hortons to "Broadcast the Brand" to customers and promote individual stores. Radio was the mainstay medium at first, when television was unaffordable. We found we could paint beautiful pictures in radio listeners' imaginations with effective, creative, and relatively inexpensive radio commercials. Today, radio advertising functions largely as a support medium for television advertising, but it remains very effective because it is so local. Unlike television programming, most of which comes from a national or international feed, radio programming is almost all done by local people for the immediate audience. The radio announcer is often a customer of the neighbourhood Tim Hortons. Well-known announcers reading the commercials or talking about the cup of coffee they brought into the station suddenly become Tim Hortons spokespersons.

Listening to the radio is such a personal activity that the content of a radio commercial can trigger an individual's imagination like no other form of advertising. In fact, stretching into the listener's imagination is almost exclusively the domain of radio, and it's a strong tool. It requires more creative work, but an imaginative radio spot can be extremely effective. When we were dreaming up radio commercials, there seemed to be endless ways to embed faith in the freshness and flavour of our products in the consciousness of our listening customers. Another advantage of radio advertising for Tim Hortons is that so much of the audience is behind the wheel. Radio commercials can stimulate an instant reaction: the customer will turn in at the Tim Hortons that's probably visible just down the road. The desire for a cup of Canada's most famous coffee is constant, and radio encourages the impulse buy.

We first attempted billboards in the early 1980s. We did our own shoot for a donut ad and happily placed the billboards in strategic locations in Ontario and the Maritimes. They didn't work. The reason was that we didn't buy enough billboard space to penetrate our markets fully, and this failure resulted from the budget problems of the times. We had actually repeated the mistake we had made a few years earlier when we didn't have the money to air our TV commercials. It wasn't until around 1995 that we decided to use billboards again, after our advertising agency convinced us to give it one more try. This time, the strategy did work. Feed back on the content of the boards worked as a support medium. Where we had used television alone for a similar product a year earlier, the inclusion of the billboards increased the sales. It worked because we rented sufficient billboards and placed them properly throughout Canada. We discovered how truly the saying "in for a dime, in for a dollar" applies to billboard advertising. If you don't saturate the markets you want to reach with billboards, they just don't seem to have an effect. Eventually, when we decided to run a campaign, we would buy over eight hundred billboards across the country.

Perhaps the most effective method of "Broadcasting the Brand" is package design. If we put the product *in* something, that package should promote the product itself. Coffee cups made our customers into walking salespeople. Proper design gave us an advertising edge with each cup we sold. This was just as true with our donut boxes, Timbit boxes, packaging bags, sandwich wraps, and yes, even our tractor trailers. These trailers became giant billboards on the highway, their colourful messages carefully tested and designed to carry the proper packaging message.

"Broadcasting the Brand" meant that we were fanatical about showing our products in print or on television, posters, or billboards exactly as they were offered in the stores. We never needed to dummy the serving size, appearance, or ingredients. We knew that we couldn't make our foods any better for the camera than what Tim Hortons served every day.

No one has summed up the principles of Tim Hortons advertising better than Miles Mattatall. "You can only eat so many hamburgers," he said. "You may not come back tomorrow for a hamburger, but people drink our coffee on a daily basis. They come back every day." This is why coffee sales grew above and beyond sales of all our other products: people could make it part of each day. Our customers appreciate the consistency of Tim Hortons food in over two thousand stores across Canada and the United States, and its advertising represents this brand consistency. Ron Joyce started it by achieving a consistent, fresh, abundant product, served in a clean atmosphere by friendly staff twenty-four hours a day, seven days a week. Our customer research confirmed that the public understands and appreciates this attitude, and that is what our advertising tries to reflect.

EFFECTIVE ADVERTISING

There's a famous expression about advertising: "Only 50% of advertising works. The only trouble is, I don't know which 50%." These days, the use of good market research, well-planned campaigns and proper media buys should tip your advertising dollars in the best direction. Here are some theories I learned about the various media.

Print

All methods of getting your message across begin with putting it down on paper. A great way to determine if an advertising campaign will work is to use the "billboard theory." You should be able to explain what you are trying to do in ten words or less like copy on a billboard. You may have room for 300 words and multiple pictures in your print advertising, but to be able to make your point, the simplicity of the ten-word approach is necessary. If you personally have to explain an advertisement, it's just not working.

Add two other items to print advertising: white space and great pictures to help sell your product or service. The old adage "White space sells" is the truth. Don't get the advertising space cluttered. Let a direct, succinct message and clear pictures do the job for you.

Packaging

I believe the most challenging format for advertising any product is its packaging. Nothing else requires more precision of thought than the package, be it a food wrapper, a box for a widget, or a health remedy bottle. The reason is that the package sits silently on the shelf and is usually the last method of selling the consumer sees. The package advertising does not change like a daily newspaper ad or a print flyer; it often has a long life in the store and then in homes or offices.

Here's an example of just how long it may take to tie two advertising mediums together. A very effective television commercial advertising a back pain remedy shows little wooden marionettes dancing away until one of them suffers a painful back spasm. The product, which I personally know lives up to its claims, relieves the pain. This highly effective commercial was widely copied, but it seemed the little dancing marionettes took months to finally appear on the product's boxes. I don't believe that the effectiveness of the television commercial was fully realized, since it was not used immediately as a reminder on the package design. The company did not get the proverbial full bang for its buck. Advance research for advertising campaigns should alert you to what should work best in print, on packaging, TV, and billboards, and in your radio messages as well. When you have that answer, you should tie all the formats together with a common message, a common visual theme. It's important to remember packaging design's longevity, because it can, as in this case, be a disadvantage. It can't be changed quickly once it is out there on a store shelf.

The familiar design of the coffee cup you take out from Tim Hortons was the result of many months of national market research, testing competitive designs, new colours, new designs, and tie-ins with the customers' attitudes about our products, and then doing it all over, again and again, until we finally got a homogenous result from the widest customer base. Much of this strategic thinking came from one individual who is an expert in this field, Barry Van Horn. For me, working with Barry gave a new meaning to seeing the light at the end of the packaging tunnel. He emphasized staying focused on obtaining the end result in package design.

Radio

Although radio uses only one of your five senses, it has the added advantage of being able to get inside your mind by letting you use your imagination. In the same way that you alone see the hero in a good book you are reading or imagine a sunset from a magazine article, radio allows people to stretch their imaginations. Imagine for example, you have the task of selling a new compact car on radio. The strategy is that it is a compact design, easy to handle around city streets yet fun to drive. Now think about developing a radio spot about this new car. Here's an idea: Our commercial starts with the sound of "Suzy," struggling to get out of her old clunker, described as a dinosaur, wedged in a cramped downtown parking lot. Bangs are heard as she describes herself exiting through the car window and throwing her briefcase on the car roof. Sure, it's over the top, but this is radio, so have some fun. Now let your imagination see the picture change as she easily parks her new compact car in a similar situation.

And what could be more enticing than party laughter heard behind the gurgling, fizzy sound of a delicious ice cold beer bubbling down the side of a frosted beer stein, all deliciously explained by an announcer as the sounds of crickets are added to the summer's night? I suddenly feel the need to pour myself one. Radio is one of the best ways of painting pictures in your consumer's mind.

Television

Here's the medium that works with two of your strongest senses, sight and sound. Where radio can let your imagination run to the limit, television fills the imagination gap for you. "Seeing is believing." Prove a television commercial's effectiveness, try this: watch a commercial with the sound off. Does the picture grab your attention? Do you know the product or service from these pictures, or is the entire commercial used as a "hook," leaving the sponsor's name right to the end? Now the next time you see this same spot, leave the sound on. Do the words really help the commercial? Does the jingle really work with the picture and message? Is the music tired before it is finished, is it a one-minute bore? And if there are words in the jingle, is the sponsors name part of the jingle? In other words, the jingle is not complete without the sponsors name, for example: "You've always got time for . . . Tim Hortons." The name of the company is part of the commercial, whether it's on radio or TV or in print. Most of all, it's necessary to show the product and service exactly as the customer will be able to buy it. It's called absolute honesty.

Effectiveness

With any form of advertising, you must ask if the message is working as hard as it can to gain the customer's interest and retain brand loyalty. No customer reads, listens to, or watches advertising for its own sake. If I really worked at it, I believed I *might* gain about 10% of a customer's initial interest. I wanted the Tim Hortons advertising to give something that was worthy of customers' time. If I concentrated on talking *to* customers, not *at* them, I might get them to come into the store. After that, the product and the service take over.

Your advertising must give customers a reason to buy. Your ads must be informative. Most importantly, you shouldn't create an advertisement that can be confused with your competitors' ads. After all, the advertisement must work for the sponsor as well as for the customer.

Most important of all, no matter what the format, I always asked myself three questions:

1. *Am I giving the customer a reason to buy the product from Tim Hortons?*
2. *Am I showing respect for the customer's time and intelligence?*
3. *Am I proving that Tim Hortons deserves the customers' business?*

Questions such as these were a useful test of the advertising I produced. Applying them to commercials for other products, I've found, can be instructive and, at times, even quite entertaining.

CHAPTER EIGHT

The True Stories Behind the True Stories

BY THE EARLY 1990S, THE DAYS OF THE TDL one-man-band marketing operation had ended. We now found ourselves with the pleasant task of finding out what people thought of Tim Hortons through the services of a research company, and then we had the added luxury of turning the creative strategy over to an agency, Enterprise Advertising (later Enterprise Creative Selling) for completion. We had added brainpower to get us to a new level.

I helped produce over a hundred radio and television commercials for Tim Hortons in my twenty-four-year career. The novelty quickly wore off, particularly with shooting television spots, which can often take up to three days and around 8,000 feet of film for one sixty-second commercial. However, the commercials in the "Based on a True Story" campaign were memorable and exciting. Like the Roll Up the Rim to Win contest, these commercials are so popular that, long after they cease to air, they remain emblematic of Canadian life. Let me take you behind the scenes of some of these productions to see how they were made and how they strengthened Tim Hortons advertising.

Lillian

I have often been asked which commercial was my favourite. "Lillian," produced in 1996 as the first "Based on a True Story" commercial, is at the top of the list. It was our first attempt to encompass in a commercial the friendly feelings people had about our coffee. The emotional responses to our product, our staff, and our stores had blended together, and our customers responded wonderfully to that sense of warmth. Putting it into a commercial was quite a feat, but with "Lillian," we succeeded. Equally memorable for me is the fact that the talent and the shoot itself were the most trouble-free of any I had ever been involved with.

In early 1996, wanting to know more about what customers thought of Tim Hortons coffee, we hired Trevor Collier Research to help us. As we learned, to our delight, how integral Tim Hortons had become to people's lives, we heard the "true story" about the little old lady who walked up the hill with her cane every morning to buy her Tim Hortons coffee. Inspired, we decided to make the story into a television commercial. Our strategic research had given us the scenario. We produced the storyboards and took them back to a focus group to see what they thought. They liked the spot, they said, but the lady looked lonely. She was walking along the street all alone. Where were her friends? They were right. The creative team went to work again, and from those comments came the friends, neighbours, and children that would surround our star with warmth.

This "true story" was true of more than one lady, and several of the similar stories came from the Maritimes. (In fact, many of our True Stories would come from the Maritimes, mainly because Tim Hortons had been a fact of life there for so many years that thousands of customers had stories to tell.) So we set off for Nova Scotia to develop the story of the old lady going for coffee into a television commercial.

As with all of our "True Story" commercials, the lead character would be a genuine customer, not an actor. However, professional actors have often depicted our hostesses because getting an amateur to go on camera and deliver the dialogue that will tie the story together can be extremely complex. Our director and agency diligently searched for just the right actress to do the speaking part. One woman who auditioned but did not get the role asked if we had discovered the perfect "leading lady." We said we had not. She said, "You should talk to my mother. She uses a cane, is in her eighties, and walks to one of your stores every day for a coffee." Our director decided to investigate.

In the waiting room sat Lillian. In the storyboard we had used the fictitious name of Mildred, but we changed it when we met Lillian. This was her real name. In her late eighties, she walked with a cane, and yes, she was a regular Tim Hortons coffee drinker. A retired choir conductor, she spoke beautifully, she had a warm smile and an effervescent personality . . . and she would have nothing to do with acting in our television commercial. She was retired, and being on camera was the least of her interests. It took our director, Michael Cerny, over a week of gentle persuasion to convince Lillian to act for us.

When the actual shoot began, we used a stand-in at first, a woman of Lillian's size and weight, dressed in Lillian's style and wearing a grey wig, though she was all of twenty-three years old. She walked through the shots so that the cameras could be set up properly. For the first time ever, we used two cameras at once in the shoot.

The specific streets of Lunenburg, Nova Scotia, needed for the

Lillian and a fisherman, setting up a shot in Lunenburg, Nova Scotia, in 1996. RB shoot were cleared for each shot. Cameras were loaded, lighting was set. We went to Miss Lillian's Winnebago, and, with the assistance of her daughter, we asked Miss Lillian to come out for her shot. Film rolled, and Miss Lillian began to walk uphill along this Lunenburg street we had selected.

"Cut!" yelled the assistant director. "That was great, Miss Lillian. Now, if you would just go back down the hill to where we started, we'd like to do it again."

"Why?" she asked.

"Just to get a little different angle."

"But I thought I did just fine."

"Oh, you did! You did! We just want to try again, for ourselves."

"Well, if you insist," said the sprightly lady.

And so it went. Every shot worked perfectly. The weather held. The background (the home of the famous schooner *Bluenose*, which we see every day on our dimes) was perfect. In the midst of shooting, we made a wonderful discovery: our perfect leading lady could play the piano, and she had a lovely singing voice.

"Get a piano!" We found one, a perfect antique. It was way out of tune. "Get a piano tuner!" A tuner was fetched from Halifax.

"Now, what would really make this work would be to have a beautiful young child sit beside her on the piano bench."

Find a child.

Up the road from our location stood one of the oldest public schools in Nova Scotia, the Lunenburg Academy, and coincidentally, Miss Lillian had gone to school there. The situation called for Superman action, and we had just the right three people to do it. First, our agency producer, Terri Black, with short-cropped black hair, trim, and standing all of five feet tall. Wearing a leather jacket with fringes and black slacks, she led the procession to the school. Her petite and attractive appearance might fool the novice, but no one could handle an agency crew, the production crew, and sundry others better than Terri. Always fair and honestly direct, she proved to be one of the best agency producers I had the pleasure of working with, bar none. Enterprise is lucky to have her talents on their side. Terri was joined by the director of photography, who had a flowing black beard and long hair and dressed as if he was ready to get on a Harley. Michael Cerny rounded out the trio. A native Californian and looking the part, with his tanned complexion and blond shoulder-length hair, he formed the tall centrepiece to the group.

Off the three of them marched, up yet another hill to the school. They knocked on the principal's door and explained that they were shooting a commercial down the street; they would really like to engage the services of one of the perfectly charming and beautiful little girls in the school. In spite of their motley appearance, they persuaded the principal, he helped them find a little girl who met their specifications, and he called her mother. Mother, child, principal, and the three supplicants from our technical staff all walked back down the street to the tangle of white trucks and cables. They had to see for themselves that we actually were filming a commercial. Reassured, the mother agreed to allow her child to be in it.

The adorable little girl had long blond hair in ringlets and wore a beautiful dress to boot. She sat on the piano bench as Miss Lillian played. Film and sound rolled. The scene was finished in just a couple of takes. We left the piano perfectly tuned.

For the next three days, all went just as smoothly, peaceful beyond what anyone could hope for. The location of the very last shot sums up just how well everything went. In this shot, Lillian is seen walking up a very steep walkway. The walkway is called Donut Hill.

At the end of many shoots, we have what is called a "wrap dinner," celebrating the culmination of what has usually been several months of work. "Lillian" followed the pattern. We took over a small dining room of a local restaurant. Normally, wrap dinners are for the crew, the agency, and the client. This time there was an exception. Miss Lillian and her daughter were invited to join us as an added thank-you. I will never forget these fine women, sitting at the head of the table surrounded by the agency and crew, all with unlit cigars in their hands (Miss Lillian, too), enjoying what had turned out to be our first "True Story."

Weeks later, the commercial had been carefully edited, with the music and sound mixed in. It was perfect. For the first and what would be the only time in all my experience of a final edit session, not one frame was changed, not one musical note varied, not one word added or removed. The rarity of commercials like "Lillian" makes them memorable, and Tim Hortons customers even today remember "The little lady walking up the hill to get her coffee."

Sammy the Dog

"Lillian" was the first "Based on a True Story" television commercial. The original nine True Stories would be made between 1996 and 2001, and more are being produced from stories submitted by our customers and store owners. All of the commercials in the series express the warmth and friendliness central to people's Tim Hortons stories.

Later in 1996, we went to New Brunswick to shoot our second True Story, which took place at D'Arcy and Barbara Murphy's store #639 on Waterloo Street in Saint John. This story was about a long-haired golden retriever named Sammy, whose claim to fame was that, every morning, he would trot from his master's store to the nearby Tim Hortons to bring back a cup of coffee, carefully packaged in a brown paper bag. Sammy's owner settled up regularly with the store staff. When we read this story in a local newspaper, we realized it was a natural for the True Story series.

This time, production did not go quite as smoothly as it did for "Lillian." The man who owned Sammy had sold the business and moved; both Sammy and his master had retired. This meant that we had to rent the store from the current owner and reset the scene so that Sammy could once again fetch his master's coffee.

On the day of the shoot, traffic had been stopped on the two streets that would be affected. Sammy was stationed inside the door of the shop. Cameras were positioned at each end of the street. Lighting, sound, and camera crews were set. The floor director called for quiet. The cameras were cued to roll, the sound was started. Cue Sammy. The director called for Sammy. Sammy would not move. He tried again, but still Sammy would not come out the door.

"Cut!" called the floor director. We went to see what was wrong with our hairy star. Sammy would only come for his master, who was with Sammy inside the store. We tried again, this time with his master outside and down the street, out of camera range.

"Quiet, everybody! Roll sound, roll film."

Sammy's master called for him. Nothing happened.

Once again, the floor director called, "Cut!"

We repositioned the shot to try once again. We discovered that, because dear Sammy was getting on in years, his hearing was not what it used to be. We found his master a bull horn.

"Stand by. Quiet, everybody. Roll sound, roll film!"

This time the master's voice boomed clearly through the bull horn, heard by all, including Sammy. Out he bounded, on his way to do his coffee errand.

Commercial shoots often attract a crowd, and this time we had more than our share. The local press had announced our coming to town, and a teacher in a nearby elementary school decided to bring her class out to see the shoot. This was fine, since the children were well behaved. The problem was Sammy, who loved seeing the kids. Sammy became a very large warm tongue attached to a very large friendly tail. We took a few moments for Sammy to greet his newfound friends, and then we all got back to work.

The second day of the shoot brought rain. This did nothing to aid the large truck that was carrying all the lighting equipment. It died an untimely death. Getting another truck was impossible — lighting trucks are specially fitted and very heavy-duty machines — so we did the next best thing. We got the company that owned the truck and the lighting equipment to hire a very large tow truck. It hooked itself up to the dead truck and pulled it wherever it needed to be for the remaining two days.

"Sammy" was completed, and our friendly dog returned with his master to their retirement. When we aired the commercial, we learned that nothing beats a story that involves pets. Then our biggest problem was that we were inundated with pictures of dogs, cats, fish, and other creatures that I'm not quite sure of, doing stunts similar to Sammy's. One dog fetching coffee is fun; in the world of commercials, more than one could be boring.

Hitching Post

In 1997, we received another interesting True Story about the special love our customers had for our coffee. An article from a Squamish, British Columbia, newspaper told about a group of horseback riders who would ride out of the mountains and down to the Tim Hortons on Progress Way, Squamish, owned by Wesley Rafuse and Kerri Lynn McArthur. The riders would hitch their horses to the hitching post outside the store and go in for their coffee. We had not yet done a True Story from Western Canada, and here was our golden opportunity: the perfect combination for a television commercial. We did the interviews, prepared the storyboards, reviewed the costs, selected the technical crew, and took off for Squamish, a small community halfway between Vancouver and the ski resort of Whistler.

"Hitching Post" was a three-day shoot. As with any outdoor commercial, weather was our master. We wanted a shot of the riders climbing Mount Garibaldi, with all the grandeur of the mountain scenery in the background. Four-wheel-drive vehicles would take the crew and equipment up the scraggily mountain roads. A special crew had taken the horses up the night before.

When the Whistler ski resort was being built, a resort was also under construction on Mount Garibaldi. A roadway had been cleared up the mountain, concrete bases for the chair lift pillars had

Shooting a "Hitching Post" scene from a railway bridge in Squamish, British Columbia, in 1997. RB

been poured, and a finished hotel stood beside the glacier. Then when Whistler was chosen as a possible site for the winter Olympics, all work suddenly stopped at this resort. The chalet had never opened, and, unbeknownst to us until the last minute, the road had never been maintained. Driving up the mountain would be downright dangerous. We desperately needed alternate transportation for the cast and crew, and we needed it now. We had to find a helicopter to fly us up the mountain if we wanted to shoot the commercial here. Not shooting in these mountains would mean we might as well have done it in studios in Toronto. We didn't have much choice. We discussed the costs and concluded that we could use a helicopter and still come in on budget.

It sounded so simple. The next morning, fluffy clouds punctuated the clear blue of the western sky. The Squamish community airport was in a valley, with mountains on either end like giant exclamation marks. Our helicopter, a large machine with a fully glassed-in passenger dome, squatted there like a giant metal bug, waiting to shuttle our people and equipment up Mount Garibaldi. The producer, key crew members, and camera equipment went first because they had to get set up for the first shot. The client (that was me) and the agency support staff would follow them.

The helicopter with the producer and crew lifted into the morning sky. It never seemed more than a thousand feet off the ground as it carved its way up the side of the mountain and disappeared into a hidden crevice. All suddenly became quiet. I watched local pilots in their Cessnas and Piper Cubs climb from the runway, and many began their counterclockwise touch-and-go practice flights. Air traffic certainly posed no problem for them. Soon we could hear distant rotors. Our machine returned, settled in front of us, and reloaded with people and gear. This time it was our turn to climb the mountain. I sat in the co-pilot's seat under strict instructions not to touch anything other than my headset. We rose as gently as a balloon on a warm summer wind. Climbing over the treetops and the Sea and Sky Highway, we began to scale the mountain range. The scenery seemed to be on a spectacular rolling scroll, as if we were stationary while it moved. The further we went, the higher we went. The helicopter's altitude above the ground remained fairly constant, and we could best understand the distance we had traveled up the mountain by looking back at the airport receding below us. Up and up we climbed. Soon we saw the crew that had gone ahead of us, perched in what appeared to be a clearing encompassed by trees and scrub. Where was the helicopter landing pad? Then we popped up slightly, and there below us was a patch just to the right of the old roadway. The pilot set the machine down on this postage stamp of sand, and we disembarked at our shoot site.

The scenery was magnificent. Miles below us, the mountainside stretched out like a living postcard. Nearby pine trees had a unique appearance: the cones pointed up instead of hanging down. We could see where the land had been cleared for the chair lift equipment. Scrub trees had sprung up on the trail. Buried deep in the underbrush were the pads for the chair lift towers. Large rusting bolts protruded from the concrete, waiting for the steel suspension frames that never came. The old unused roadway, a grey incision cutting into the side of the mountain, stretched down from where we stood, making a series of sharp turns toward the chalet. The paint of that never-used building had withered in the harsh mountain climate. Through binoculars, I could make out dining room tables, which appeared set for a dinner that would never be served. Time had stopped for this ski resort.

Food on a shoot is always important. No matter what the location, food, water, and the necessities of life must always be provided. There is method in this madness. Crew breaks are relatively short, the longest usually a single one-hour dinner break per day. If the crew disappeared into a Lunenburg diner or went shopping in downtown Saint John, the schedule would disintegrate and leave the shoot in total disarray. Excellent catering is a vital component in keeping the shoot on schedule and therefore on budget.

So how would we eat on top of a mountain? Around eleven a.m., the helicopter made one more trip up the mountain with the catering crew on board. They produced pans of hot food, covered with lids and aluminum foil, from the flying machine and served it on an old, half-hollowed-out log that lay beside one of the paths. A hungry cast, film crew, and client partook of the fare, made even more delectable by the crisp mountain air.

We maintained radio contact with the little Squamish airport at the bottom of the mountain. Bad weather would set in later that day, so we had to begin our aerial shoot on time. Equipment was packed, horses with their riders had begun their descent, and the passengers lined up to board the helicopter.

Mine was one of the first flights back down. The pilot told us we were flying heavy, not exactly what I wanted to hear. The rotors whirled away, and we slowly became airborne. Actually, that is almost a falsehood; we flew only about five feet above the old roadway. As we rose, the rotors cleared the trees on either side by inches, leaving them angrily pushing away from us under the rotors' thrust.

Although I am a seasoned air traveller, I was about to experience a new sensation. As the helicopter moved slowly down the old roadway, I could have disembarked without a step, we were that close to the ground. Suddenly, when the road turned sharp right, we did not. We kept going straight over the edge, over a chasm that suddenly dropped thousands of feet below us. It was a toe-curling sensation, sitting there in the co-pilot's position, looking straight down through the glass under my feet at what transformed from a comfortable roadway to . . . nothing. I looked up and concentrated on the distant horizon to regain my stability. Below us, wildlife scurried from the roar of the engine. As we had come up, we went down, our altitude determined by our descent. In the distance, the airport beckoned. The mountain loomed behind us, the day's shooting safely in the film cans.

Mountain climbing with a helicopter was not the only interesting form of transportation on the "Hitching Post" shoot. The cast and crew would also remember the fate of a motorcycle and its errant young driver. A certain shot would be taken from a railway bridge. looking down the grandeur of a river. We set it up, aiming the equipment toward the distant shoreline beneath us. We cued our horseback riders to proceed into the ford there.

Stand by. Roll Film. Cue performers . . . and action!

Stop camera. Stop performers.

Some kid was testing the attributes of his noisy cross-country motorcycle. I don't think he knew we were shooting a commercial, since the camera was so far away from the horses he was encircling. He just wanted to see what confusion he could cause the riders.

Zoom! Down the shoreline he drove his machine. Zoom! Up the shoreline. Zoom! Around the horses. Zoom! Down the shoreline. Sploop! He disappeared in a spray of hissing water at the edge of widening rapids. The engine bubbled to a quiet death. The machine began to do lazy rollovers in the deepening, rapidly moving waters. The kid spluttered to the surface and crawled up on shore. The bike disappeared, never to be seen again by anything but fish.

We learned later that the young man had taken this brand-new motorcycle out on a test ride from a local dealer, who had no idea where his machine was going. The driver did not own the bike. He walked back, wet, to the dealer with, as Desi used to say to Lucy, "some serious 'splaining to do!" The shoot restarted without further incident.

"Hitching Post" proved to be a spectacular commercial. Truth in advertising is far more than just showing the product in a totally honest light. In this case, we could have faked the mountains, not used the actual Tim Hortons in Squamish, and cut other corners to save money. If we had, we would have lost the real reason for coming out west to shoot this commercial. Just as the coffee, the donuts, and all the other food products are real in a Tim Hortons commercial, so are the True Stories surrounding them.

Natalie MacMaster

Many True Stories came from our customers or the store owners, but two of the best came from the insight of Patti Jameson, Vice-President of Corporate Communications.

The first commercial she suggested was shot in 1997. It revolved around Natalie MacMaster, the Cape Breton fiddler, who was on her way to becoming an international star. Patti had seen Natalie perform at an Atlantic Provinces store owners' convention. During her show, Natalie had mentioned how much she loved Tim Hortons and told how she and her crew made a point of stopping at Tim Hortons whenever they could on their tours across Canada. Patti echoed the sentiments of Gary O'Neill: they thought this would make a great True Story. Putting together this commercial was a joy, since Natalie is a true professional. She was always ready to go and always cooperative, even at two o'clock in the morning, when the shoot was finally completed.

Natalie's commercial worked because it reflected the true grit of a Canadian performer. The commercial was based on her real life, showing a True Story about a fine Canadian who shared her love of Canada and Tim Hortons. This commercial, like the other True Stories, reflected what we had come to realize about our products. Tim Hortons was not just a product but a part of people's lives.

Kuwait

"Kuwait," the other True Story that Patti brought to the table, involved HMCS *Toronto* on maneuvers. The story came to Patti's attention through the Department of Defence. In 1998, when Art Eggleton, Minister of National Defence, was planning to visit the troops in Kuwait, his staff asked, "What can we bring from home?" The answer: "Tim Hortons coffee!" Officials contacted Patti, and she quickly complied. At the same time, she asked if a camera crew could go along to record the handing over of the coffee. We received permission, and a crew did what is called a "guerrilla shoot": the cameraman also captured the sound, and the director took nothing more than basic professional equipment. They shot unscripted, unrehearsed footage, much like a home video. The results were spectacular.

As we edited the commercial, we realized that we were missing one key line said by the seaman who was the spokesman. As luck would have it, HMCS *Toronto* had returned to Canada and was moored in Toronto. The ship was there and so was the crew — all except our seaman. He had stayed home in Halifax with his wife, who was soon to give birth. We persuaded him to fly to Toronto and record the one missing line on board the ship. The line was completed, cut into the final version, and the commercial was perfect.

Shorty

On air, these commercials look so easy, but the minute details and the huge expenditure of time necessary to make them just right are seen only from the other side of the lens. We did two more True Stories in 1999, shot back to back. This schedule made for very tight production times, but because of the seasons and the weather, they had to be done close together.

The first involved Shorty Jenkins, a professional maker of curling rink ice surfaces all over Canada. His story came to us from a bonspiel in Nova Scotia. As Shorty built the ice surfaces, he seemed to live on Tim Hortons coffee. He was pleased to tell the local store owners about his love for our coffee, particularly because the local store owners were supplying the product. He said he timed the layers of ice by his trips to and from the nearest Tim Hortons to get his coffee.

"My hat's pink, my curling shoes are pink, my phone's pink. My favourite colour's pink!" Shorty provided his own script. He was one of the few True Story characters whose unique phrasing and unusual speech patterns were actually recorded as part of the finished commercial. However, all was not quite perfect. The reason: we "assumed." Never assume.

We filmed the commercial in North Bay, Ontario, because that was where a curling rink was available in a beautiful northern city that gave the right atmosphere to the commercial. We needed shots of people curling, and we assumed that, when we got to North Bay, the ice in the arena would already be down, including the white base and specific markings for curling. It takes considerable time to start a curling surface from scratch, and we did not have a lot of it. A thin coating of frozen water over the bleak concrete floor confronted us. White tape could be seen clearly, zigzagging over the concrete, and the cast and crew stood around at our expense. Everything came to a grinding halt, including my patience.

Darcy Maloney, the creative director of Enterprise Creative Selling, solved the problem. Since there was a little ice, we had something on which to slide a curling stone. Darcy simply changed the camera angles to shoot from the ice surface slightly up toward the curlers, rather than down toward the ice surface. Add some mist on the ice and presto! A great shot. Shorty, with his pink hat and happy, rapid-fire speech, gave us a commercial that became so popular it was satirized by the CBC's Royal Canadian Air Farce.

Surfer

We went directly from North Bay to a beach outside Dartmouth, Nova Scotia. We had read in a magazine that Australians came to Nova Scotia in the winter months to surf, incredible as that may seem. The article mentioned Tim Hortons coffee as a great discovery and a necessary part of the Australians' early morning surfing routine. We found surfer Lance Moore and his surfing shop, just as the article described them. Lance would appear on camera, speaking about his adventures with the Australians in this unique Canadian surfing story. I had a concern, though. How could we differentiate the Nova Scotia surf from the surf in California or Australia? Water is water. We did not want our viewers to think we had invented this by dropping in stock footage of kids surfing on the beaches of California.

Our creative team found the answer in a small fishing village that shouted "Canada." To make it even more Canadian, we added a Canadian flag to one of the huts. We didn't think anyone would really notice the Nova Scotia plates on the old pickup truck, but we were glad they were there. We had trouble finding an actor with an Australian accent, but, unknown to us, we had one with us in our technical crew. An Aussie through and through, he had a "down under" accent that was sometimes hard to understand. Again, we took advantage of what we had by encouraging our new-found actor to use his own lingo, and we superimposed standard English on the screen. Unplanned as it was, this "translation" added a wonderfully authentic flavour.

This was the first time that I saw a performer wear different hats in the literal sense. Our lead character had a baseball cap he used when moving equipment, and when he was to appear on camera, he changed his cap for an Australian-style hat. With his accent, there could be no question that the commercial featured an Australian in Canada.

Unscheduled Stop

In 2001, we added a locomotive and freight train to our marketing history: a True Story in which a locomotive engineer stops his train near a Tim Hortons store, jumps down, and rushes in for extra-large coffee "to go!"

The True Story of "Lillian," aired in 1996, spawned an avalanche of interest from our customers, who recounted their own tales of the lengths to which people would go for a Tim Hortons coffee. This particular story about the locomotive engineer actually came from several different sources and several different locations throughout Canada. The problem with making the story into a commercial was that stopping a train for this purpose is apparently against the rules of the major railways.

What we needed was a private railway line where this had really occurred. Eventually, we got lucky. We heard about a railway line owned by the town of Orangeville, about forty miles north of Toronto. The town uses the line for servicing commercial accounts along a thirty-mile stretch of track that runs, in part, through the beautiful Caledon Hills. It also runs within a hundred feet of a Tim Hortons which is owned by Paul Preuss. The engineer often did stop while he and some of his crew nipped in for a coffee. Our commercial, to be named "Unscheduled Stop," could now begin.

As always, what appears easy at the outset can soon become infested with little problems. One glitch was the fact that the train went in only one direction. There were no turntables or rail loops at the ends of the line, so when the train completed its run, the engine simply went in reverse and pushed it backwards. We solved this by simply "flipping" the negative when we wanted the train to go in the opposite direction. However, when we did the shots, we had to make sure that everything in the picture would read properly when it was flipped: there could be no lettering or names, and numbers had to be reversible, like "101."

Flipping a negative may sound like a detail that only the agency should be concerned with, but I believe it is just as important for clients to know about these challenges. On packaging, the wording and numbers must work anywhere the commercial might be shown. In a price-point commercial, the creative and the copy must work together in such a way that prices can be changed in different marketing areas. The more clients know about these technical points, the more capable they are of offering an extra set of eyes on a shoot to see that such details have all been covered. The intention isn't to find errors but to ease the way to a superior final product. The smoother the production, the more cost efficient it becomes for both client and agency.

Darcy Maloney, who put the winning touches on many True Story commercials, allowed me to work closely with him and his team. Usually, clients are kept away from an agency's creative team for fear, I believe, of stifling them by expressing creative ideas that could make some clients legends in their own minds. In our case, they put up with me, often letting me work side by side with the team to help them transfer the feelings of Tim Hortons professionally to camera and microphone.

During the "Unscheduled Stop" shoot, I felt that the train took on human characteristics. For the exterior shots of the train going down the track, we used a specially equipped half-ton pickup truck. Its road wheels had been replaced with railway wheels, so it could go up and down the track. On the back of the truck, a special platform held the camera and crew. One shot required our truck to start nose-to-nose with the locomotive. On cue, the train would back up while we in the truck moved in the opposite direction. In the commercial, the film would run backwards. A train would

Shooting "Unscheduled Stop" in Orangeville, Ontario, in 2001. The crew is working on a flatbed pulled by a pickup truck with railway wheels. RB come at viewers with lightning speed, and just at the moment of "collision," the commercial would cut to the next scene.

To make this near-collision work, we cued the engineer to start or stop the train with a walkie-talkie. Instead of saying, "Okay, start the train," our director called the engineer by name, saying, "Okay, Bill, you can start now." From our vantage point, however, we could not see the engineer, Bill, just this 640-ton locomotive bearing down on us. Sometimes the train would be a mile down the track, completely out of sight. On cue, the train began the action obediently, as if it were human. Sometimes I though my mind was starting to go after too many commercials.

This spot was a technical breakthrough, in that we used no voice-over to tell the story. This, too, was one of Darcy Maloney's brilliant ideas. For the first time, we had a commercial visually effective enough to make words superfluous. The train stopping, the engineer coming into Tim Hortons and getting coffee for himself and his crew — these images needed no verbal support. The quality of the coffee and the strength of the brand name came through in the story itself: this product is good enough to stop an entire train!

Coach

How could we talk about Tim Hortons and not talk about skating? We couldn't. In 2001, I had been invited by the CBC to see a hockey game in the Air Canada Centre in Toronto. At the end of the first period, I got up to stretch my legs when the arena announcer began to talk about a children's hockey team called the Tim Hortons Timbits. I turned around and saw about two dozen kids come skittering out from the far corner entrance of the ice. Their little legs moved in a blur as they began to chase the puck dropped by their referee. Nets had been set up at the blue lines. Down they came, totally wrapped up in their game, oblivious to the thousands of fans who, like me, had stopped and turned around

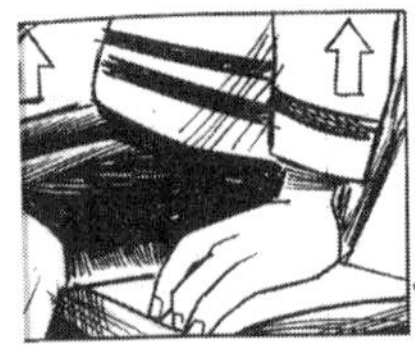

Working sketches from the "Coach" pre-production book. TDL / SPARKS PRODUCTIONS to watch. The crowd got behind these youngsters with boisterous applause and roaring cheers. The blue on white and white on blue Tim Hortons Timbits uniforms had taken over this professional arena. A goal was scored! The horn sounded! Cheers rang out! A commercial idea was born.

Gary O'Neill started the Timbits hockey teams in Moncton, New Brunswick. Naming the little hockey players who would wear the Tim Hortons shirts Timbits, after the famous little round donuts, made perfect sense. The idea was expanded upon and continued to grow under the guidance of Kathie McPhee, the regional marketing manager in the Oakville marketing department. Instead of sponsoring one or two teams, Tim Hortons worked through the local stores to develop Timbit leagues for boys and girls aged nine and under, with some players as young as five. They all gear up safely to enjoy Canada's national sport, dressed usually in combinations of company colours — red on white and white on red, or brown on yellow and vice versa. Blue-shirted Timbits play against white-shirted Timbits, and so on. Kathie promoted Timbit games as entertainment during the intermissions of professional games in major arenas. To go to these professional games, teams are chosen from Timbit leagues close to the arena, bused in on the Tim Hortons courtesy bus, and have the fun of playing alongside the professionals. This outing costs the children and their families nothing, and it's very exciting for the boys and girls who play, not to mention the parents who accompany them. And after the game, the kids and adults are treated to — you guessed it — Timbits.

Timbit games had been taking place for several years in the Air Canada Centre, but the only people who had seen them were the lucky ones right there in the arena. The national television cameras don't pick up the kids' games, since the networks already have commercial commitments and other programming to show during the intermissions. We were doing research on some of our food products at the same time as we were thinking about the merits of doing a commercial about the Timbits kids. We decided to take the story boards for this commercial — we were calling it "Coach" —

to focus groups, tag them on at the end of the sessions, and see if the idea of these little kids playing hockey at the Air Canada Centre would interest our customers. The focus groups' responses eliminated the doubters, including the person running the research, who initially said, "It seems this idea is coming from the bottom up and not the top down." Overwhelmingly, every man and woman in every group waxed nostalgic about everything from the late Tim Horton to playing hockey when they were kids to their own kids. In particular, they mentioned the Tim Horton Children's Foundation and its good works. This was interesting, since the kids' camps had nothing to do with the subject under discussion. The focus group results predicted a winner.

We began working on "Coach" with one requirement: the players seen in the commercial had to be legitimate Tim Hortons Timbits team members. We did not want child actors because the True Story had to be true. So we went out and found a team willing to participate.

The story line was based on a coach talking to his players in the dressing room before they went out on the ice, telling them they should "always remember where they came from and enjoy the game." It was a great way to introduce the reality of these Timbit teams to all of Canada. The difficulty was that the commercial would take three days of shooting with some very young children. We wanted to make sure, above and beyond union requirements, that they and their parents or guardians did not get unnecessarily tired or stressed. As it turned out, the kids had more stamina than their adult companions and the members of the crew.

We shot all the footage in the Air Canada Centre with their full co-operation. We spent one day in a dressing room, one day on the ice, and the final day shooting the actual game in front of a live audience of real hockey fans who had come to watch a Leafs game. All three days went well. On the night of the game, the children arrived in the underground parking area on the Tim Hortons courtesy bus and went to their special dressing room. The kids and their guardians were treated royally.

Four huge professional movie cameras had been set up in the arena to record the Timbit action: one in the press box high above the crowd, another halfway down in the stands, one in the penalty box looking toward the gate where the kids would come out onto the ice, and one just inside the gate itself, out of sight of the other cameras. As usual, the director controlled the cameras using walkie-talkies, but this time, the walkie-talkies failed just before shooting began. We had to rely on the fact that the cameramen had been fully prepped and knew which shots to get. The little Timbits came out on the ice on cue and skated their hearts out. They seemed almost oblivious to the huge crowd and concentrated on their own game in a fabulous facility. Like the Timbits in the first game I saw, they were at least as popular on the ice as the pros during the real game. All of the cameras worked perfectly, and they got excellent footage.

"Coach" proved to be one of the most popular commercials we ever produced. It was a learning experience for all of us because it didn't fit into the normal pattern of promoting a defined product or service, which is the usual reason for spending money on commercials. Viewers saw not one donut, not one cup of coffee, no cups, no product identification. Only the company logo appeared at the end of the commercial. All the copy, including the great tag line, was written by David Wallen, from Enterprise. "We never forget where we came from" at the close of the spot says many things to many people about Tim Hortons and especially about their own past. We had produced our first corporate commercial, promoting the company's attitude toward children and its support of community spirit. Inadvertently, "Coach" also reflected the feelings surrounding the Tim Horton Children's Foundation.

Shooting a "Coach" scene on the ice at the Air Canada Centre in Toronto. The camera is on a sled that can be pulled by a skater. RB

The True Stories campaign continues, with commercials showing over and over how Tim Hortons has become part of many people's lives. Ron Joyce would often say, "The harder we work, the luckier we get." Not every time at bat is a home run, but Tim Hortons has earned a very high batting average, thanks to hard work and the luck hard work brings. The effort put into developing the brand has been accepted so warmly and understood so clearly by our customers that they have responded by providing our True Stories, and these commercials have, in turn, worked their way into the nation's culture.

CHAPTER NINE

Changing Times

IN 1985, ROLL UP THE RIM TO WIN was not the only dramatic change for Tim Hortons. In October of that year, Paul House started with the company as my boss in the Marketing Department. He was hand picked by Ron Joyce with the obvious intent that he would eventually take on the role of President and Chief Operating Officer. Paul filled the bill with more people than just Ron. Like Ron, Paul had been with Dairy Queen, but he began his retail career selling produce from his mother and dad's Ontario farm. Each week, before he drove off to the Saturday market, his dad told him, "Don't come back with anything on the truck." He didn't. He learned his retail skills from his family, and he capped off his education with a

Store	Location	Opening
1	Hamilton, Ontario	1964
100	Thunder Bay, Ontario	1978
200	Waterdown, Ontario	1984
300	Calgary, Alberta	1987
400	Halifax, Nova Scotia	1989
500	Alymer, Quebec	1990
600	Beamsville, Ontario	1992
700	Moncton, New Brunswick	1993
800	New Glasgow, Nova Scotia	1994
900	Trois Rivières, Quebec	1994
1000	Ancaster, Ontario	1995
1100	Westaskiwin, Alberta	1995
1200	Lachine, Quebec	1995
1300	St. John's, Newfoundland	1996
1400	Pontiac, Michigan	1996
1500	Pickerington, Ohio	1997
1600	Kanata, Ontario	1998
1700	Port Colborne, Ontario	1998
1800	North York, Ontario	1999
1900	London, Ontario	2000
2000	Toronto, Ontario	2000

The Tim Hortons chain grew from its first location in 1964 to 2000 stores by the year 2000.

degree from McMaster University in Hamilton. Today, he still lives on a southern Ontario peach farm.

Some things you just can't teach. One of them is the great ability to be brilliant and still communicate easily with the common person. Paul is that kind of man. Doug Poad, who was a vice-president with Enterprise Creative Selling, once said that Paul House is the kind of guy who could ask you to charge up Pork Chop Hill with nothing more than a pea shooter and you'd want to ask when you could leave. When he steps onto a podium, it doesn't matter whether there is one person or 1,500 in the audience; Paul eliminates the distance between the microphone and the listener. He and Ron made a great team. Ron said once, in a light-hearted manner, that it took him thirty years to get the first thousand stores, but it took Paul only five years to get the next thousand. Paul would reply that he had started from a strong base in the first thousand stores, and he achieved his thousand-store increase because of synergy, a strong support staff, and great franchisees. In actual fact, if a company doesn't have a Ron Joyce or a Paul House waving the baton, nothing gets done, at least not done well. The Tim Hortons chain grew from its first location in 1964 to 2000 stores by the year 2000. It did not happen overnight, but growth escalated as the years progressed. The success of the business was matched by the development of the Tim Horton Children's Foundation. As the number of stores increased so did the need for children's camps to serve and return a service to these communities.

Paul House advised store owners on more than one occasion, "Be aware of the changing customer." It's necessary to keep up with the times, to keep presenting customers with the variety of new items they want. In the same vein he would state that he would rather "have a lot of little problems" — with getting a new product or service going — "than one big problem" — it doesn't sell at all. Sage advice.

Bill Moir, Executive Vice-President of Marketing, expresses the same message more succinctly: "Customers like new stuff." This somewhat tongue-in-cheek remark acknowledges the necessity to continue to change some of the ways in which Tim Hortons products and services are offered.

John Hoey, who is a multiple store owner in and around Mississauga, Ontario, took diversification to heart. Stores literally wear out after seven to ten years of service and must be upgraded. One of his stores was due for remodelling, and yet John wanted to keep it operating. He came up with the idea of renting a trailer. He had it hauled in and left it at one side of the parking lot. Next he fitted the trailer out as a store, with entrance and exit doors, a take-out counter and shelf display, and a small kitchen area. A simple excavation into the parking lot revealed the necessary water and sewage lines. Electrical hookup came from the street pole, and it was "business as usual" at John's Tim Hortons as the renovations on the original store got underway. John's customers appreciated having the store remain open, and John appreciated the customers' staying with him while he was rebuilding. Clearly, John was of the same mind as Paul House, who likes to point out how much easier it is to keep a customer than to go out and get a new one.

In Niagara Falls, Ontario, Alec and Wilma Strom varied this theme slightly when they rebuilt one of their stores, #34 in the system. They had the space behind the existing store to build a new store, so they didn't actually renovate. They simply started over again. The old store operated as usual, and when the new store was completed, the old store, now standing in front of the new one, was torn down in about a day. Alec and Wilma had a new store and an enlarged front parking lot as well.

When a store on Appleby Line in Burlington, Ontario, required renovations, the owner devised another change on keeping business going. He simply rented the nearest available space, which was in a small strip mall just across the road, and moved his business there temporarily. It worked. In fact, it worked so well that this second location remained in operation as a "satellite" after the original store was refitted. A satellite is a location without the set-up of a full kitchen. The product is supplied from the main store and finished with icings and decorations at the satellite location. This

Burlington owner discovered that he had made it just as easy for people going southbound to stop in at the satellite as it was for those going northbound to stop at the main store.

In the early years, Tim Hortons was often asked to provide a portable store for special events. This assignment is harder than it seems. Coffee, the keystone, requires a ready supply of clean, fresh water. This does not mean hooking up a garden hose to someone's outdoor tap. In many cases, it means that, in order to operate a portable store, a tanker truck of fresh drinking water must be brought in. Electrical power for heating the water and refrigerating the cream and other dairy products had to be available. Washing facilities for our staff and for the kitchen and serving area was an absolute necessity. In other words, we had to be able to put a store on wheels if we were going to supply the high quality food and service that our customers had grown to expect.

A properly trained staff was the most important necessity of all. A portable store can be left in a back storage yard when it's not in use, but with staff it's a different story. Often, we had to bring trained Tim Hortons staff from a main location to work in the portable store, thus short-staffing the permanent location. After years of trial and error, we produced a properly operating portable store, and several of these units are in operation now, all driven by requests from our customers.

In Hamilton, people often comment that it seems there's a Tim Hortons "on every other corner." We were often asked why we opened so many satellite stores and whether having many stores decreases each store's potential.

As TDL grew, new property would come up for sale in cities

in which we did business. These lots were often close to existing stores. Simple mathematics comes into play. If the parent store is making X dollars at a certain location, will a satellite simply divide the business in two, adding extra operating expenses while decreasing the sales at the parent store? The concern proved unfounded; the second outlet added more business when the sales of the two stores were combined. This simple example shows why. The largest selling item is coffee, and people will stop at the nearest Tim Hortons for a coffee. Remember, you don't make a reservation to go into a Tim Hortons. The products are high impulse buys, and therefore extra locations did not seem to affect the business of existing stores adversely.

This proliferation of stores proved to be a big help when the company decided, years before it became law, to stop allowing customers to smoke in the stores. The change succeeded because multi-store owners in Hamilton, one of the first cities to introduce this policy, would make some stores non-smoking and allow smoking in others. The different rules divided the customer base: smokers went to one location and non-smokers went to another. This made the switch to a chain-wide no-smoking policy easier to implement, since in most cities, we were already halfway there.

Smoking is literally a dying pastime. Smokers appreciated the freshness in our non-smoking stores, and they liked the convenience of going to the closest location, which as often as not would be a non-smoking store. With the decline in the number of smokers, plus the cultural change that accustomed smokers to going outside for a smoke, the non-smoking stores became predominant, and finally the entire chain became non-smoking before it was a legal requirement.

Varying the way we did business led to one of the more interesting Tim Hortons store designs. Called "Double Drive Thru," it features no sit-down area and no kitchen, just serving windows on either side of the small building, plus a walk-in, stand-up counter. Only the hot beverages are prepared on site.

Initially, regular stores built in drive-through windows so the customers could place their orders and receive them through the driver's window. Not all stores could accommodate this driver-side drive-through construction; some driveways and right-of-ways allowed a drive-through to be placed only on the passenger's side. This seemed so counter-intuitive that TDL management was reluctant to okay a store owner's request for such an arrangement.

Not wanting to disappoint the owners, however, we investigated methods of delivering food to the passenger side. One way of doing that involved an enclosed conveyor belt that would carry the food over the vehicle and lower it to the driver's window. This contraption proved just too slow and awkward, and then payment was equally awkward. Customers had to send money back to the store on the conveyor, and often they had to wait for change. The conveyor idea was quickly dropped.

The first "Double Drive Thru" was built in Oakville, near the head office. Two menus and speaker systems were set up, one operated from the driver's side and the other from the passenger window. Similarly, the order and pickup windows were built on either side of the little building to hand over the order and take in the money on the side from which the order had been placed. The idea worked. When we could compare the percentage of business that would go through the passenger side to the percentage that would go through the driver's side, we were able to supply hard facts to our owners.

Anne Murray sings a Peter Allen song, "Everything Old Is New Again," and I had the opportunity to learn that lesson well. In the late 1980s, an advertising agency produced two slogans for us that seemed to work: "Always fresh, cause you keep eating them" and "Always fresh, cause you keep drinking it."

A donut box from about 1965, bearing the "new" slogan "Always fresh," displayed at the TDL head office in Oakville, Ontario. RB

We had used "Always fresh, cause you keep eating them" in several television commercials for donuts and cookies. It seemed like a natural extension to put it on the coffee cups. There was one small problem. Actually, it was a big problem. The line was too long to wrap around a take-out coffee cup, and this became even more difficult when we made the line bilingual. It is almost impossible to translate English advertising slogans directly, word for word, into French, and vice versa. Here is one of the closest translations we could use on the take-out coffee cup: "Always fresh cause you keep drinking it" became "Toujours frais parce que vous n'arrêtez pas de le déguster," literally, "Always fresh, because you don't stop savouring it." Needless to say, if one line followed the other, we'd need to use ridiculously small type to make them fit around the circumference of a cup.

I went with just the two first words: “Always fresh / Toujours frais.” This would fit on the cup, and it described all of our fresh-made products more than adequately. The slogan is still used today, and now it appears with the Tim Hortons logo as well.

On display in the company’s head office is the original donut box designed by Ron and Tim. When I took a close look at it, I discovered some interesting facts. The cardboard was strong enough to keep its shape if it had been filled it with nails. Copy is everywhere, but there are no pictures. And there, on one end of the box, is the phrase: “Always Fresh!” And I thought I was so original. Ron and Tim were more than twenty years ahead of me.

Changing times bring new ways of advertising. I had tried for some time to get a space to advertise our company on the rink boards at Maple Leaf Gardens. One afternoon I received a call from William J. (Bill) Cluff of Maple Leaf Gardens Ltd. Bill and I had spoken several times in the past about our interest in MLG rink boards. Now space had come up on a corner position, and Bill needed an answer before the end of that business day. The rink boards had great exposure to the audience watching hockey on television, particularly this corner position. Actually, we would receive two boards, the one that would appear on camera and the one on the diagonally opposite corner, seen only by the fans at the game. The opportunity sounded ideal. I immediately began to call all the voting store members on the advisory board for their approval to spend the funds on this new program. From west to east, they agreed unanimously. In one afternoon, with the aid of Ma Bell, a decision to go ahead with this new advertising format was reached.

I called Bill Cluff back and agreed to his offer. There was one ironic twist to our deal. When this program was being put into place, Bill's ultimate boss was Harold Ballard. Bill told me that Pal Hal had only one stipulation: we had to generate twelve post-dated cheques to cover the one-year contract. It was the first and only time that someone asked Tim Hortons for post-dated cheques. Maybe Harold thought the chain was still struggling. Fortunately, we were past that level now. The cheques were generated and we were now on Maple Leaf Garden rink boards; soon our advertising would appear on the boards of many other professional arenas across the country.

In 1975, the Tim Hortons Children's Foundation had just set up the Tim Horton Memorial Camp, in Parry Sound, Ontario, and Tim Hortons acquired its first bus. A decrepit converted 1960s school bus, its purpose was to take children to and from the camp. In 1979, the company replaced it with a new MCI highway cruiser, complete with washroom, that would carry forty-seven passengers in smooth, air-conditioned comfort. While the main purpose of the bus was to serve the children's needs in the summer, it was used off-season as a courtesy bus for groups who could not afford to pay for a regular bus. Senior citizens' homes and other charitable organizations made use of it. As the years went by and the budget increased, a total of four buses were purchased to serve the needs of the additional children's camps across the country, and these provide no-charge courtesy bus service as well. Tim Hortons buses are now stationed in Calgary, Oakville, Montreal, and Debert, Nova Scotia, not far from Tatamagouche.

Having purchased these buses, the company wanted to get as much positive exposure from them as possible, particularly in the winter months when outside organizations didn't seem to need them as often. How could we vary the use of the bus?

For years, we had wanted to join the parades in our communities; Santa Claus parades and sports parades were very big, especially in Toronto and Hamilton. To the curbside crowds and the television audience, a large highway bus would lack the appeal of an elaborate float, but we could not afford a float. How could the bus become a float?

There was no manual to tell us how to turn a bus into a parade float, and the attempt posed many challenges. The bus had to remain safe and viable for its primary purpose, taking passengers safely on the highway, so we could not drill into it or add hooks, pulleys, or wheels that had to be left in place after a parade. I had no more knowledge of highway buses than I had had of paper cups, and I knew even less about making our highway cruiser into a rolling, self-propelled parade float.

I began by going around and around the bus, looking for anything that could support signage other than paper posters. Finally, out came the stepladder. Around the entire top edge of the bus was a rain gutter! It would serve admirably. Hanging signage could be attached, using bungee cords hooked to the gutter and the frame underneath the bus. Bungee cords hooked large wooden discs to the wheels, and these discs showed pieces of sports equipment — pucks, baseballs, footballs, basketballs — that rotated as the cruiser moved slowly along the parade route. It made one of its first excursions in the 1980 Grey Cup Parade in Toronto, promoting "Canada's Good Sports."

From this "bus float" concept sprang another advertising idea. One of our most popular products, then as now, is Timbits. A cartoon mascot of this product had been designed composed of three Timbits: two as "ears" and one as the "body." Little flat feet and big cartoon eyes were added to bring the character to life. From 1974, when the Timbit product line was first introduced, to the mid-1990s, the little character was seen in much of our advertising. I was always intrigued with how the people at Walt Disney had

The Tim Hortons bus, which could be converted in about one hour into a parade float, in the 1983 Grey Cup parade. In front of it are four Timbit mascots and the helpers who walked alongside to protect them. Two of the Timbit characters rest on wagons. RB

turned their cartoons into walking mascots. Eventually, we found a manufacturer of these items in Toronto. The tiny Timbit character soon became a giant that could walk along in parades or around stores as a special attraction.

These first walking Timbits had a few problems. Made mainly of cloth, with harnesses to support the considerable weight on the wearer's shoulders, these outfits could be worn for only about forty-five minutes at a time. Wearing the Timbit became a nightmare if it got wet, and disaster could strike when rambunctious children or disruptive teenagers decided to use the Timbit as a punching bag. I spent many hours on a golf cart, winding through various parades, supervising the walking Timbits. When they walked beside the bus, "walk-alongs" helped guide and protect them. Someone would even pull along a small wagon to serve as a portable rest station for the tiring Timbits. They could sit down on the wagon and wave sedately at the passing crowd, and in this way, we could keep them mobile for longer periods.

In the mid-1980s, a sales rep wanted to show me a new type of outdoor advertising, an inflatable product that could be designed to look like just about anything. The sample he showed me was about four feet tall and depicted a 35mm film can. The thing had a small fan outside the unit, attached by an umbilical-style air tube that constantly blew into the "film can," and lights inside illuminated it. I was so impressed that I immediately ordered one to be built just like our Tim Hortons take-out hot drink cup twenty feet tall. When it arrived, I had it set up on the front lawn of the head office, where everyone could see it. We plugged in the fan and turned on the inside lights, and suddenly a giant Tim Hortons coffee cup nestled into the second-story window, right beside Ron Joyce's office. Fortunately, he, too, was impressed, and we soon had several to send around to stores for special promotions.

As the sales rep was leaving after completing the first sale, he said, "Oh, by the way, we make a portable one, too, that can be worn outdoors." Bingo. Soon the old cloth Timbits went to that Big Bakery in the Sky, and the new, lightweight, portable Timbits, complete with a battery-powered fan inside, soon graced parades and special functions with willing staff members inside.

Eventually, public tastes changed so much that the Timbit mascot no longer received instant recognition; it had to be explained to the public. In fact, successful as the walking Timbits became operationally, the public always had difficulty identifying them with our product. Often, as I supported one of these characters in a parade, I would hear a mother tell her child, "Look at the giant mouse, dear!" By the mid-1990s, the time had come to drop the Timbit character from our advertising.

The original 50-cent gift certificate, about 1988, and a one-dollar gift certificate, about 1998. RB

It's hard to believe today, but there was a time when Tim Hortons did not sell gift certificates. The organization consisted of franchises, with over ninety per cent of the stores owned by independent operators licensed to use the Tim Hortons name, products, and services. If store owner A sold a gift certificate, and the customer used it at a store belonging to owner B, then A would have the money, while B had provided the product. How would B get paid? The finance department eventually solved the problem, but, quite apart from practical challenges, initially Ron Joyce didn't receive the idea warmly. He didn't see the need for gift certificates. Even so, I believed strongly that if we offered gift certificates, our regular customers would give them to a lot of people who were not necessarily already customers. Gift certificates would bring new customers through our doors. The discussions among Ron and me and the store owners continued for about a year.

On Christmas Eve 1987, I was still working. Everyone else had gone home, or at least I thought they had gone home. The stillness of the empty office was suddenly broken by the ringing of my phone. It was ringing on an inside line. It was Ron. He, too, was obviously still in the building, in his second floor office.

"Ron."

"Yes, sir," I replied.

"I just had a couple of calls from customers. They wanted to know if we sold gift certificates. I think you'd better get them started."

I don't know who those two customers were, but they kick-started an item that is one of our most popular sellers all year round, but particularly at Christmas. Initially, coupons were issued at a value of fifty cents each in books of five. Next, they went to a dollar each in books of five. Finally, we began to produce both Canadian and American gift certificates in one- and two-dollar denominations. These have benefited the customer: they're a convenient gift, and they allow customers to treat friends or business associates to a fresh donut, coffee, or sandwich at the recipient's convenience. They have also benefited Tim Hortons: they increase the stores' cash flow by generating add-on sales, and they draw in new customers, often for the first time.

It was clear from the beginning that Tim Hortons take-out cups were one of the company's most important advertising vehicles. It was also clear that drivers often turned into a Tim Hortons store on impulse, got their beverage and snack at the drive-through window, and continued their trip. Combining these facts pointed out the value of making it easy to drink a hot beverage in a vehicle.

By about 1985, we came up with an idea for making our ordinary paper cup into a travel cup: the Timtote. This little gem was equipped with two stainless metal spring clips on the inside. When you pressed the paper cup into the holder, the clips held it right in place. It didn't move around, it didn't fall out. The Timtote even came with a little base to attach to the car dash.

So where are Timtotes today? We had to stop producing them because the cost of the little Timtote was more than the customers wanted to pay, even at a break-even price. The metal clips had to be manufactured and manually inserted, and then the unit had to be assembled. It was requested and preferred by the customer to "double cup."

Back in December, 1977, one of my first projects had been to introduce the Tim Mug, the brown plastic cup with a stick-on base that soon graced so many Canadian dashboards. In the early 1990s, when we decided to produce another exclusive Tim Mug, it seemed logical to try and make our famous eight-ounce original crockery mug into a travel mug. I tried one of these mugs in several different car cup holders. It appeared that, with modifications to the handle design, a plastic model would work as a travel cup. It would need a drink-through lid and a separate base that could be attached to the dash of vehicles without a built-in cup holder. A lid design was chosen; it would be produced in red. The mug itself would be bone white, with a raised red logo, and the little base would also be red.

More than three months later, the moulds were ready. The plastic pellets were loaded into the moulding system, the buttons were pushed, the moulds clamped together and released, and our little mugs, lids, and bases came bouncing down a rubber-belted assembly line. Engineers stood at the end of the run and checked the first mug off the line. It appeared perfect. Next came the lid. It, too, was without flaws. When they cooled, we successfully snapped the lid on the cup. Finally came the little red base. The engineer slipped the base on the bottom of the mug and then, using two hands, handed over the mug with lid and base attached. He needed two hands because the base would have dropped off the bottom of the mug if he had not actually held it on. Over the din of the plant machinery, I tried to explain that this would not do. The base had to stay on the bottom of the cup by itself, just snugly enough that, when it was attached to a car dash, the mug could be easily removed. They thought they had a perfect fit, but finally I convinced them that we wanted to sell these three pieces together as one, with the cup full of coffee. Therefore, we could not sell it with the extra wrapping or blister packing necessary to hold the base to the cup.

"This will mean a complete remake of the cup mould base," one engineer said. "Can't do this and get the project finished on time," said another. "We'll have to adjust the inner ring of the cup to fit tighter to the ring in the base. Won't be easy to get it right without a warp factor," said yet another engineer.

A young man stood on the catwalk beside the great moulding machinery, listening to our animated conversation over the roar of the plant equipment.

"I can fix it," he said.

"And how would you do that?" asked one of the design engineers incredulously.

"With a slot-head screwdriver," he responded.

"Come on down and show me what you mean," I said.

Down he came, his slot-head screwdriver in hand, and, taking the first white mug that had come off the line, he flipped it over, revealing two concentric rings. One ring was the outside edge of the cup, the second was an eighth of an inch inside it. He placed the screwdriver in the slot between the two rings and gave it a slight twist. He did this in three equally spaced places around the rings, forming slight indentations. These, we discovered, acted like a tread or grip on the single ring of the base as it slipped between the rings on the cup.

The manoeuvre worked. Within the next hour, the giant mug mould was disassembled, and four small notches were cut into the steel, one more notch than in the hand-made sample. When the new test unit emerged from the machinery, I took the assembled Tim Mug outside the plant and tossed it high in the air. It did not come apart. The bumps that young man created became a permanent part of our new Tim Mug.

I have this first of over a million Tim Mugs with me today. If you are among the many Canadians who still own one of these white Tim Mugs, you can turn it over and see the small notches for yourself.

CHAPTER TEN

Building Memories
The Tim Horton Children's Foundation

DEVELOPING STRONG COMMUNITY ROOTS contributed strongly to the growth of the company. One important way in which Tim Hortons put down these roots was by means of the Tim Horton Children's Foundation, which supported summer camps for monetarily challenged children.

The first Tim Horton Children's Camp began soon after Tim Horton's tragic death on February 21, 1974. The sudden loss of the company's co-founder was deeply felt by Ron Joyce, his partner, and the store owners who knew Tim. He had great affection for children. Although he shied away from the publicity spotlight that shone on him as a star NHL defenceman, he always participated

The Tim Horton Memorial Children's Camp at Parry Sound, Ontario. TDL

wholeheartedly in anything related to kids. In memory of this love for children, Ron founded the Tim Horton Children's Foundation in the year of Tim's death. This non-profit charitable organization is committed to providing an enriched and memorable camp experience for economically disadvantaged children and youth. It extends Ron's belief that a company should give back generously to the communities that support it.

The Tim Horton Children's Foundation was built to fulfill the dreams of those who remembered Tim and the dreams of thousands of children who wanted the chance to enjoy a first-class summer camp holiday. It had simple beginnings, just like the Tim Hortons chain. Operating strictly from donations, it had no great amount of cash on hand. Over the years, hundreds of Tim Hortons staff and store owners have given time and energy to make sure the camps continue to be an important part of the company.

The foundation's mandate is to select eligible children wherever Tim Hortons stores are located. Going to camp costs the children and their families nothing. All air and ground transportation, accommodation, food, camp activities — every expense, from the moment they leave their homes until they are escorted back — all are covered.

The first site was an old fishing camp on Lorimer Lake, north of Parry Sound. It had a lodge with a large stone fireplace, a kitchen and main dining area, and some smaller rooms for the staff, and it also had (and has) a beautiful sandy beach. Near the beach were four small cabins or "bunkies" for the guests who used to come to the camp on fishing trips. Since these "bunkies" were really designed for summer use, they offered no real protection from cold winds or winter temperatures.

In the early spring of 1978, I joined many others at the camp on one of the many work weekends organized to get the site ready. The volunteer work party consisted of TDL staff and anyone else who wanted to help out, and on this weekend we would help build, clean, install, and paint the camp site to make it suitable for the kids.

It was cold. I slept in one of the bunkies, and I do not recall ever having been so cold. The winds came swirling in from Lorimer Lake and attacked the slat walls of the bunkhouse with a monstrous vengeance. A red-hot space heater and every piece of clothing that I had brought, including my coat, could not keep out the penetrating cold.

I rose early the next morning, anxious to get started, if for no other reason than to get my circulation going again. Ron himself, far more energetic than most of us, prepared and served breakfast.

The old bunkies soon became a part of the camp's history, one of the first parts of the old fishing camp to be levelled. One of the initial projects was to build two large, deluxe sleeping cabins for the forty-five children who would attend each of the ten-day sessions of summer fun. Between these two cabins were separate washrooms and showers for boys and girls. Docks were built for

The original camp bus, from the first issue of *Tim's Times*, the company newsletter, August, 1976. TDL

the growing flotilla of paddleboats, sailboats, and canoes. At either side of the entrance road, raised stone arms were erected, recreated from the Tim Horton Children's Foundation logo.

Professional cooks and trained directors were hired to run the camps each summer. They would hire assistants to work with them, often students studying in a similar field. Food supplies would be ordered, often from the head office, with fresh milk and eggs purchased locally.

In the early camp days, I was one of the people to order groceries and fill the shelves for the kitchen. So how do you know how much groceries you need to feed forty-five hungry kids three square meals a day for ten days? I started with a box of corn flakes. Asked to figure out just how many boxes of corn flakes would be required as just one of the breakfast items, I went home, took out a box of corn flakes, filled a bowl, and discovered that two ounces made a generous serving. From there I calculated that a large box of corn flakes would provide about thirteen servings.

I kept at the multiplication and realized we would need a lot of corn flakes. Better get some Cheerios, too. Bacon, eggs, fresh breads, toast, juice, milk, porridge, pancakes, and lots of seasonal fresh fruits joined the cereal choices. Lunches and dinners were just as resplendent.

We went to a local fruit and vegetable market before each camp session to load up cases of fresh produce, and I soon gained great respect for the strength of people in the fresh fruit and vegetable business. Corn, tomatoes, potatoes, cabbage, lettuce, bananas, apples, and peaches are all very heavy, and each box got heavier as I swung them into my car or the Tim Hortons bus.

The original Tim Hortons bus, a converted school bus, was painted in the camp colours, blue and white, with the Tim Horton Children's Foundation logo centred on each side. The bus conversion consisted of extending the end of the passenger compartment by about ten feet to accommodate a chemical toilet and additional space for luggage. The one thing the converters forgot, however, was the gasoline tank. It held about ten gallons, which meant we had to stop about every half hour to refill it. Air conditioning consisted of dropping the side windows. The kids provided all the entertainment with their sometimes-on-key singing voices. It was great fun.

In the early days, here's how a typical camp session would begin. I would pick up our two bus drivers, store owner George McGlinchey, one of the original owners, who had purchased store #9, and his friend, A. J. Thompson, both of whom were in the Cambridge area. This saved them having to leave their cars at head office in Oakville while driving the bus to the camp. I'd get on the road around four-thirty in the morning, pick up the drivers, head back to Oakville, and see that the bus got to the fruit market to pick up fresh supplies. Our aim was to be at the camp on Lorimer Lake around lunchtime.

Various pickup points were arranged, including Tim Hortons parking lots, schools, and shopping plazas. When Tim Hortons stores opened in Buffalo, kids were brought up from there to Toronto so they, too, could join the fun. We'd start out with juice

The Tim Horton Children's Camp at Tatamagouche, Nova Scotia. TDL

and snacks at Tim Hortons, of course. As we headed north with the two drivers, chaperones, luggage, food supplies, and forty-five very excited kids, we soon heard, "How long till we get there?"

"Half an hour!" George or A.J. would reply.

This would continue all the way up north. No one seemed to question the fact that the half an hour stretched to three hours. Soon the bus drove through the raised stone arms at the Lorimer Lake camp entrance and deposited the children at the lodge.

Peter Moffat, the Lorimer Lake camp director from 1981 to 1991, would say to the children, "Take all you can eat, but eat all you take." Peter, a former NHL referee, had started his career as a children's camp director in the United States, running camps for the YMCA. When he came to the Tim Horton Children's Foundation, he had over twenty years' experience behind him. At the camp sessions, he and his wife, Cheryl, would put on "Christmas in July" with all the trimmings: turkey, Christmas pudding, and Santa Claus, too. Many of Peter's original programs and ideas are still used today at all the foundation camps.

When the kids were packing up to go home, they were given a fresh new camp T-shirt to wear. Often, they would neatly fold them into their travel bag (which might consist of no more than a green garbage bag or an old pillowcase) and take them home as a special souvenir.

One time, we took a child back to the schoolyard drop-off point, where he was to meet his family. No one came. I waited in my car for half an hour to make sure he would be okay, but no one showed up for this little nine-year-old boy. Finally I went over to him, picked him up with his belongings, and drove him directly to his home. The man who answered the door didn't seem to care whether or not his son was back. He had forgotten to pick him up.

When pressure of time made getting up to the camp difficult for staff or store owners, one of the company aircraft, a twin-engined Gruman Widgen, would be called into service to transport these no-charge helpers. This amphibious aircraft would take off on wheels from Hamilton Airport and land on Lorimer Lake.

Landings and takeoffs on the water were rather difficult, so it was not used to transport children. The Widgen was first manufactured in the 1940s by the Gruman Aircraft Company for use by the United States Navy in air-sea rescue. Fans of old TV shows will recall that, at the beginning of each episode of *Fantasy Island*, a Widgen would descend as one of the characters shouted, "Da plane, boss! Da plane!" If that doesn't ring any bells, picture yourself standing on one water ski. This would compare to the fuselage of the plane, sitting on the water. Now extend your arms out to the sides like airplane wings, and hold a broomstick with a small float on the end in each hand. These represent the two pontoons that

Camp des Voyageurs Tim Horton at Quyon, Quebec. TDL

keep the wings from tipping into the water during landings and takeoffs. If you feel awkward standing like this, imagine how a pilot feels when trying to fly this craft.

One of the Widgen pilots was Barry McSween, who had piloted the twin-engine Beechcraft Duke on that fateful trip to Thunder Bay for the opening of the hundredth store. He was at the controls of the Widgen when it made a memorable landing on Lorimer Lake with two visitors to the Tim Hortons Children's Camp. Barry had been asked to take two senior Ontario store owners to the camp, Len Graham, from Kitchener, and George McGlinchey, from Cambridge. Len, a barrel of a man who looks strong enough to lift a car with one hand while changing the tire with the other, is a kind and gentle person whom I have never seen out of sorts. George, one of those laid-back, happy people who doesn't let much of anything get him down, faces life with a genuine smile. Both men would be tested.

McSween said that the Gruman Widgen had originally been equipped with twin 200-horsepower Ranger engines. Thus it was somewhat underpowered for a six-passenger aircraft that needed to pull itself out of the water like a mechanical porpoise. Emil Meshberg, another of the company pilots described this porpoise action more succinctly. During a water takeoff, the nose of the plane actually goes under the water, causing the pilot's vision to be completely obliterated. Count to six, he said. If the pilot still couldn't see, the plane was sinking. This particular aircraft had been upgraded to twin 370-horsepower Lycoming engines. Although it had over fifty per cent more power, Barry said, the bigger engines also changed the plane's centre of gravity. This made landings and takeoffs even more difficult.

Barry's flight up to the camp with Len and George had been uneventful. Barry made his approach, gently touched the fuselage to the water, and proceeded to throttle back. Just then, the right wing pontoon caught a wave, causing the plane to do what is known as a water loop: it spun violently around, ripping off the pontoon and puncturing a hole in the wing, which dipped dangerously into the water.

Immediately, Barry ordered Len and George to get out of the aircraft, crawl up onto the left wing, and counterbalance the sinking right wing. Len, large as he is, scrambled through the plane, out the hatch, and onto the wing as if he had been practicing the stunt all his life. George hesitated a bit. He couldn't swim. However, faced with the choice between drowning in the plane and taking a chance outside it, George decided on the latter course and scampered out onto the left wing.

From shore, it was quite a sight. Here were two grown men perched on the far end of the wing, legs dangling, fingers clamped to the leading edge, with Barry revving both engines. The twin propellers kicked up a mighty spray. Barry jockeyed the throttles that hung down from the ceiling of the cockpit with one hand while manoeuvring the steering yoke with the other. With the two human counterweights on the wing, he managed to bring the plane across 1,000 yards of water and safely up onto the shore. Len recalls laughing through the adventure, whereas George recalls the experience rather quietly.

In the early days, forty-five kids were invited to Lorimer Lake for each ten-day session throughout the summer; about 270 kids per year could attend camp. Today, Tim Horton camps accommodate 4,200 kids each summer for ten-day sessions, and another 4,800 day campers attend at the same time. The day campers can stay over for up to three days at a time, with their own special programs and huge teepees in which they enjoy a good night's rest. That's 9,000 children every year.

Having some campers return to camp was an idea that intrigued Ron Joyce. Now, through a series of Youth Tracking Programs under the guiding eye of the president of the foundation, Don Schroeder, children from thirteen to fifteen years of age who benefit greatly from their original camp experience and show promise are invited back to participate in the Wilderness Adventure Program, a six-day wilderness canoe trip. Like their original trip to camp, their Wilderness Adventure costs them nothing. The program gives special kids who excel at camping and group activities the opportunity to grow through deeper and broader experiences.

The next step is the Leadership Program for fifteen-to-eighteen-year-olds who have successfully completed the Wilderness Adventure Program. These young people are invited to participate in leadership development, life skills training, community work, and internships. They go back home with computer skills and the ability to write a resume, and they take a copy of their work home on a CD, all at no cost to themselves. The Tim Horton Children's Foundation wants to give them an added boost to help them really succeed in their lives.

Organizing air and ground transportation has become a very big part of the foundation's activities. The coordination of buses, airlines, and local pick-ups can be quite a challenge. Late planes and suddenly changed schedules call for creative thinking about how to entertain the kids while they wait to go home or catch up with the rest of the group. In 1978, an airline strike grounded planes throughout the country. Not one to be turned back in the face of adversity, Ron Joyce brought out the company turboprop aircraft and took five young girls home to Halifax.

After one camp, I had to drive a few of the children down to Toronto ahead of the Tim Hortons bus so they could catch their flights home. One of the boys had brought along his new-found pet, a very large bullfrog called Freddy. There the two of them sat, in the centre of the back seat, the boy and his frog. His camping companions sat on either side, and two other kids were in the front seat with me. I knew that my young friend couldn't possibly take his frog back to his city home. The other children agreed, and together we persuaded this boy that it would be best to leave Freddy in some Ontario waters. Going over a bridge, we spotted a marina that bordered on a beach surrounded by reeds and stopped the kids all walked to the water's edge and deposited Freddy in the warm, reedy pond.

Over the years, the Children's Foundation grew, and Tim Hortons had stretched across Canada and into the United States. The largest group contributing financial support has always been the Tim Hortons store owners. Once a year, owners give the proceeds of their coffee sales for one day to the Tim Horton Children's Foundation. Customers put the money into a special donation box on the counter, and they may add their own contributions to these boxes as well. Customers knew about the camp in Parry Sound,

The Tim Horton Children's Ranch at Kananaskis, Alberta. TDL

Ontario, and eventually they began to ask, "Why am I donating to a camp that is thousands of miles from where I live? Why shouldn't I be supporting kids in my own neighbourhood?"

They were not alone in their queries. One by one, more camps were built to serve the needs of more communities. The foundation acquired additional campsites, professional staff members, and highway coaches. But the spirit remained the same. The various suppliers to Tim Hortons cover over 85% of the food and equipment costs, and the store owners and customers remain the biggest financial contributors. In 2002, the one-day donation of coffee sales raised over $4.8 million for the camps, more than $2 million of it being gifts from customers. That's a long way from the $25,000 a year collected in the donation boxes in the early 1980s.

Golf tournaments for store owners and Tim Hortons suppliers, held each year in Kananaskis, Alberta; Quyon, Quebec; and Tatamagouche, Nova Scotia, as well as on Ontario courses that have included the famous Glen Abbey course in Oakville, have become very popular fundraisers for the camps. Together, coffee days and customer donation boxes, golf tournaments, and support directly from the store owners make it possible to cover the $10 million operating costs to run the camps each year.

Another goal of the foundation is to give children a chance to discover other parts of Canada, and now the United States, by visiting a Tim Hortons camp distant from their homes. Kids from the East Coast are often flown to Ontario, Ontario kids are taken to Quebec, Quebec children may fly to Western Canada, and children from Kentucky might go to the Kananaskis Camp, near Calgary. There are now six Tim Hortons Children's Foundation camps: Tim Horton Memorial Camp, Parry Sound, Ontario (1975); Tim Horton Children's Camp, Tatamagouche, Nova Scotia (1988); Tim Horton Children's Ranch, Kananaskis, Alberta (1991); Camp des Voyageurs Tim Horton, Quyon, Quebec (1994); Tim Horton Camp Kentahten, Campbellsville, Kentucky (2001); and Tim Horton Onondaga Farms, St. George, Ontario (2002).

The success of the Tim Horton Children's Foundation camps reflects the original philosophy of Ron Joyce and Tim Horton: be fair in your actions and give something back to the communities you serve. This success reflects the same attitude on the part of store owners, suppliers, and customers, who express their faith in this philosophy through continuing contributions and support.

At work at my home office. TED BRELLISFORD / COURTESY OF *THE HAMILTON SPECTATOR*

CHAPTER ELEVEN

Summarizing Success

TIM HORTONS STARTED WITH NOTHING MORE than a dream, a few dollars, and personal values that came from starting life during the Great Depression: the willingness to work as hard and as long as the job required; the acceptance of the principle that, to spend a dollar, you had to have a dollar; and the drive to make the most of whatever resources might be at hand. Supplying neighbourly service and great donuts and coffee twenty-four hours a day, seven days a week, with consistent high quality in every single store have made Tim Hortons a part of Canadian life.

Ron Joyce's business savvy and Tim Horton's stability and foresight set the company on the path to success, but Ron himself has admitted that he "had no idea just how far we were going to go." From the very beginning, the individual store owners' successes had a synergistic effect, attracting others who wanted to become franchisees and join the team. Ron says, "The success of this chain is really due to the hard work and combined dedication of the franchisees."

Tim Hortons changed radically between my first day of work, on November 13, 1977, and my retirement on December 31, 2001. When I started, I was the entire marketing department for seventy-nine stores, and my budget was, in today's terms, almost invisible. The challenge of achieving big results from small investments always stimulated my curiosity and creativity and made my job immensely exciting. My personal objective has always been to take everything I learn today and put it into making a better business day tomorrow.

Roll Up the Rim to Win reflects my own attitude and the attitude of Tim Hortons. In 1967, I worked with large rolls of paper to make a finished product: four-inch-wide rolls of photofinishing paper to make Black's Bigger Prints. In 1986, the large rolls of paper were ten-inch-wide poly-coated paper cup stock. The success of the Roll Up the Rim to Win advertising campaign has been gratifying, and the contest has become a defining part of Canadian life. Yet the simple qualities that have made Tim Hortons what it is today made it possible for the light to dawn at that fateful meeting with the Lily Cup sales rep on September 4, 1985. These values left the minds of the company owners open to moving forward with a contest that a richer or more conservative organization might have dismissed. They have also made it possible for a single advertising campaign to gain strength every year, even after seventeen years.

After spending twenty-four years as the Tim Hortons Marketing Director, I can't help but try to assess the reasons for the company's phenomenal success as it appeared to me, from the vantage point of my own desk. Encapsulating this success in a dozen points is an interesting challenge.

Fairness

The mission of Tim Hortons is to be fair to the franchisees and the customers alike. Over 90% of the stores are owned by franchisees, but the company is in the business of selling businesses, not just franchises. TDL wants franchisees to succeed, and there is no "us against them" mentality. Payment of a franchise fee is only the beginning of a very fair relationship with TDL. New franchisees are thoroughly trained, and if a franchisee's senior store management needs upgrading, Tim Donut provides training at the facility in Oakville that is second to none. If a storeowner has trouble with his profit-and-loss statement, Tim Donut is there to help. At the Tim Hortons head office, the mandate is to respond to every call from a store owner as soon as possible but certainly within twenty-four hours.

Customers are the key to any business. Tim Hortons listens to customers on a continuing basis, through direct customer comments and through focus groups that include, not only Tim Hortons customers, but people who like other brands as well. I've always thought that a company that doesn't listen to its customers might as well close the doors and go home. TDL has found that listening and acting on customers' advice is a fair way to be sure of going in the right direction, and it's also a path to better sales.

Giving Back to the Community

The Tim Horton Children's Foundation, a combined effort of management, store owners, suppliers, and customers, is a perfect example of "giving back." Over the years, as more promotional materials about the camps appear in the stores, more customers learn about what the foundation does for underprivileged children. Knowing about the Tim Hortons policy of giving back, with no strings attached, they have the opportunity to join in, creating more community strength.

Timbit sports programs work for children throughout the country, with many hockey, soccer, and baseball leagues totally sponsored by Tim Hortons. Store owners help others by donating products and services to various organizations. And Tim Hortons courtesy buses provide needy groups and charities with free transportation.

Chain Strength

There is strength in numbers. The larger the number of stores, the greater the buying power. A purchaser of coffee for over 2,000 stores has a lot more bargaining power than a purchaser for a single shop. As the chain grew, so did the advertising fund. More dollars meant more advertising on radio and television, in print, and on billboards. We could work continually at improving our packaging designs.

As the strength of the chain grew across the nation, an interesting phenomenon developed at company conventions. The formal presentations were always well attended, but the personal time, in which franchisees relax and get to know one another, offered great learning opportunities. Store owners from one part of the country soon discovered that challenges they thought exclusively theirs had been met by other owners. The size of the chain provided more answers for the owners simply by getting everyone together.

Thinking Out of the Box

The belief that everybody is creative, that other people's ideas are worth listening to, that no one should be afraid to bring up or try new ideas — these have been operating principles for Tim Hortons. Once, when I made a presentation about a new hardware product to a group of store owners, one of them said to me, "Ron, I think the idea is nuts. I'll take 500 and give it a try." I can't remember whether he was right or I was. In any case, that kind of positive attitude helped us all on the pathway to success.

The Roll Up The Rim to Win program was totally original, a completely "out of the box" idea. Even though it had not been done by any other company, TDL and the Tim Hortons store owners gave it a try. The rest is history.

Selling Finger Food

Tim Hortons started as a seller of snacks. Not a pre-made snack, sealed in a bag or wrapped in plastic, and not a chocolate bar, but a fresh snack. Except for soup (which you can drink if you want to and not use a spoon), all of the company's biggest successes are foods that you eat with your fingers: donuts, Timbits, muffins, cookies, sandwiches, bagels, croissants, and, of course, fingers wrapped around a cup of Tim Hortons coffee. Our customers have made these finger food decisions for us. They want food to eat on the go, food that's easy to serve, food they can buy quickly at a drive-through window.

Taking a Break

When we first began our market research studies, we wanted to understand our competition, but the only studies available focused on quick service restaurants serving things like hamburgers. There were no extensive records on companies like Tim Hortons in Canada. We actually built a whole new category of food service business.

At Tim Hortons customers often go for "a coffee and a donut, and maybe I'll have another coffee, and my friend will have a cookie, another donut, and could I get a fresh coffee, please?" The local Tim Hortons became the place to go for coffee breaks, and then it became synonymous with coffee breaks, or work pauses, or a stop after taking the kids to the dentist, or any time people just want a few moments to themselves with a great cup of coffee. It's true: "You've always got time for Tim Hortons." Tim Hortons is there, 24/7. Customers come as they are, order what they want, and stay and enjoy or take their treats with them.

Product Consistency

One of the best compliments Tim Hortons receives is, "I travel a lot. I always know that your products are consistently good, no matter which city, province or state I am in. A ham sandwich or a cup of coffee — it's always just as good, from one location to the next."

Consistency sounds easy, but it takes a lot of continued hard work to figure out how to do it, and it takes a lot of work to achieve it everywhere, every day. It starts with development, and that sophisticated Tim Hortons research and development lab makes the food taste right to begin with. Keeping it that way necessitates constant testing of raw materials, such as flours and mixes, that come in from the suppliers, and most importantly, a top operational crew to monitor and assist the store owners throughout the chain.

Everyone at Tim Hortons knew from the beginning that quality had to be at the forefront. For example, the company wrestled to produce a menu of excellent sandwiches at the lowest possible cost. In the end, the testers selected ham, tuna, roast beef, and breads of the same quality as customers served at their own dining room tables. The products have to be just that good. Cheapness is never a compromise.

Recession Resistance

The very nature of the business gives it a built-in advantage. In 2002 the average Tim Hortons sale was approximately $2.50. This seems to be affordable, even when the economy takes a dip. Like the vast majority of restaurants, Tim Hortons took its biggest decrease in growth in 1992 with the introduction of the Goods and Services Tax (GST), but other than that, the company has weathered many a financial storm simply because of the nature of its business. Taking the principle further, the soup and sandwich combinations offer a good light meal and a beverage for about $6, an excellent value at any time.

Pleasing the Customer

The original store on Ottawa Street, Hamilton, was a converted gas station. You could catch your clothes on some of the inside walls, they were so rough. It was a start. Next came the famous brown brick on both the inside and outside walls. This decor was fine as long as the fashion lasted, but it began to look dated when tastes changed.

Ron Joyce would say, "We're the best of a bad lot" — the old-time coffee-and-donut shops. Others had set the pattern: dark, late-night hangouts, filled with cigarette smoke and offering stale donuts. Tim Hortons was in the shadow of the competition. Ron wanted to break that stereotype, retaining the convenience in a cleaner, friendlier atmosphere. He and Paul House accomplished this feat with a strong store design department and carefully chosen locations, such as universities and highway roadside stops. TDL insisted that owners maintain well lit, clean parking lots, in front of the store wherever possible. The original customer skew was 55% male : 45% female. When we brightened up the stores, added new colours, improved the uniforms of the staff, increased the lighting in the parking lots as well as in the interiors, and ensured that the

My daughter Suzanne taking home a box of donuts, 1982. RB

washrooms were safe and clean, women visited Tim Hortons in far greater numbers. And when we expanded beyond donuts, both men and women appreciated the new menu. We took one step at a time, but all the time, we were listening and improving the chain for the benefit of our customers.

Research and qualitative focus groups give guidance; the participants' comments are just that. Tim Donut Ltd. must cull and modify and make decisions that fit within the framework of what the company wants to do and can do for its customers.

Promoting from the Inside

Tim Hortons started with very little financial backing, and we learned to make a little go a long way. This was a great benefit to the growth of the company. For many years, advertising outside the store was a luxury. New foods had to sell over the counter first before advertising was considered to make sure they appealed to the customers.

We found advertising through package designs to be one of the most effective and cost efficient ways to develop the brand. The brand had to work first, because what we learned from knowing the product, what we learned from talking with customers, was expressed in the package design and colours. Each customer became a messenger for Tim Hortons as he or she went out the door. Eventually, the packaging appeared in media promotions as well.

Sometimes companies include media promotion at the product launch, but all the commercials in the world will not make the cash register ring if the product is not up to snuff. Tim Hortons soups are a good example of this. Some soups sold better than others. Some sold better in some parts of the country. They were all up to our usual high standards of quality and flavour, but the variety needed to be refined. Before advertising soups nationally, we made sure we were promoting the types most popular right across the country.

I like to think of a store being the "inside" advertising format and the media being the "outside" format. Once the "inside" is just right, the media portion becomes easier. Conversely, using the media to promote a product that customers don't like will lose the customers. In the trade, it's called "over-promising." No commercial can make up for a substandard product, but if, through research programs and focus groups, the advertising agency has done its homework, a customer-proven product will be a winner for sure.

Being First

Since Tim Hortons was unique, it has been first many times, but the theory of "first in wins" works only when a company offers the right products and value. Often, having the right products and services will put a company in first place even when a competitor appears to have won the race.

Being first is related to the out-of-the-box conception of new ideas and services. Just because something hasn't been done before doesn't mean it can't be done. Think positive. Give it a try. Tim Hortons has aimed to be Number One: first on the block, first in quality, service, and value, first with new ideas. Nobody remembers Number Two. It's important to know what the competition is doing, but I've learned that if you look over your shoulder too much, you'll run into that unseen wall in front of you. And if you come to the marketplace after a competitor, you must be better in all respects. Customers appreciate quality, service, and value above everything.

The KISS Principle

"Keep it simple, stupid" is a phrase I heard more than once from Ron Joyce. Once I got over taking it personally, I realized that simple, clear thinking throughout our programs worked. Tim Hortons has one superior brand of coffee in the stores; the stores make one great coffee and make it the best. No pots of multiple flavours sit around getting stale at Tim Hortons. There's just one great coffee. It's a consistent brand, and it stays around no longer than twenty minutes. This is the ultimate demonstration of the KISS principle.

A donut is a donut is a donut, a fun product that people should enjoy. Keeping the promotions for donuts in this vein lets customers know that Tim Hortons isn't trying to make donuts into something else. Keeping it simple respects people's intelligence.

In an interview in August, 2002, Brenda Bouw, then Enterprise Editor of *The Hamilton Spectator*, asked me what I considered my greatest achievement. I answered, "To have been in the right place at the right time by being invited to join the team at Tim Hortons. It was the right time to grab onto the tail of one of Canada's most successful business comets and learn how to fly!"

This cartoon originally appeared in *The Calgary Sun*. DAVE ELSTON / ARTIZANS.COM

Notes

CHAPTER ONE
Grabbing the Tail of a Comet

Additional information was obtained from Eddie Black, Sr., in various personal conversations, 1968-1970; an e-mail interview with Bob Black, March 8, 2003; and a phone conversation with Henry Svazas on February 28, 2003.

CHAPTER TWO
In the Beginning: Who Put the Dough in the Donuts?

My information for this chapter was supplemented by interviews with Jim Charade on November 19, 2001, and February 12, 2003; Jeri-Lynn Horton Joyce, February 16, 2003; Ron Joyce's nephew, Graham Oliver, February 19, 2003; Ed, Florence, and Miles Mattatall, February 14, 2003; and John Lynn and Jim Flemming, November 11, 2001. The figures on franchise fees are from an article in *The Hamilton Spectator*, July 27, 2002. I also compared information received from my informants with *Open Ice: The Tim Horton Story*, by Douglas Hunter (Toronto: Viking, 1994), pages 255-256.

CHAPTER THREE
"We Were All Like Family"

Information for this chapter came in part from interviews with Ed, Florence, and Miles Mattatall, February 14, 2003; Eldon Fawcett, January 21, 2002; and Gary O'Neill, February 25, 2003, and from *Tim's Times*, March, 1977.

CHAPTER FOUR
Going Coast to Coast

Additional information was supplied by interviews with Art Jenkins, February 17, 2003; John Lynn and others, November 11, 2001; Paul Preuss, November 11, 2001; Bud Kennish, December 5, 2001; Eldon Fawcett, January 21, 2002; Ron Fitchett, January 3, 2002; Bruce Leckie and Stan Hare, TDL warehouse staff, February 26, 2003; and Wilma and Alec Strom, March 2, 2003. Facts and figures on the American operations are from *The Toronto Sun*, February 1, 2003, and *The Toronto Star*, February 12, 2003. Karen Wilson's

December, 2001, letter to me helped refresh my memory. Details of Tim Horton's death are taken from public records as well as from my discussions with Lori Horton and from the book she co-authored with Tim Griggs, *In Loving Memory: A Tribute to Tim Horton* (Toronto: ECW, 1997). The stories about the exchange between Ron Joyce and Bud Kennish, Tim Horton as a ditchdigger, the flipped plans, and the truck with automatic transmission were told by the participants at company events and in a CHCH TV interview with Ron Joyce at the opening of store #200 in December, 1984.

CHAPTER FIVE
My Partners, the Store Owners

Conversations with Barry McSween, on April 11, 2002, with Alec Strom, on March 1, 2003, and with Peter Moffat, on February 28, 2003, added to my information about the events described. I also found valuable information in *Tim's Times*, December, 1978.

CHAPTER SIX
Roll Up the Rim to Win: Eight Years to an Instant Idea

"Horton Hears a Boo from Customers" is reprinted from the *Toronto Sun* with the permission of the author, Steve Irwin.

CHAPTER SEVEN
Broadcasting the Brand

My recollections for this chapter were supplemented by conversations with Angelo Mosca, December, 2002; Donna Lloyd, April 10, 2002; Jack Kuper, March 3, 2003; and Miles Mattatall, February 14, 2003.

CHAPTER EIGHT
The True Stories Behind the True Stories

I am grateful for extra information supplied in conversation by Kathie McPhee, March 6, 2003.

CHAPTER NINE
Changing Times

Bobby Baun mentions advertising on rink boards on page 252 of his book *Lowering the Boom: The Bobby Baun Story* (Toronto: Stoddart, 2000), by Bobby Baun, with Anne Logan.

CHAPTER ELEVEN
Summarizing Success

At various staff meetings and conventions and in personal conversations over the years, Ron Joyce, along with senior staff, including Paul House, Bill Moir, and Henry Svazas, expressed their beliefs as to the chain's success. I have paraphrased some of their thoughts and added my own theories.

Index

C

D

E

F

G

M

N

O

P

Q

R

S

T